S0-CBS-588

Developments in Animal and Veterinary Sciences, 1

GUIDE DOGS FOR THE BLIND: THEIR SELECTION, DEVELOPMENT AND TRAINING

Developments in Animal and Veterinary Sciences, 1

Guide dogs for the blind:
their selection, development, and training

CLARENCE J. PFAFFENBERGER
JOHN PAUL SCOTT
JOHN L. FULLER
BENSON E. GINSBURG
SHERMAN W. BIELFELT

with the editorial assistance of
Sarah F. Scott

ELSEVIER SCIENTIFIC PUBLISHING COMPANY

AMSTERDAM · OXFORD · NEW YORK   1976

HV
1780
S4
G84

ELSEVIER SCIENTIFIC PUBLISHING COMPANY
335 Jan van Galenstraat
P.O. Box 211, Amsterdam, The Netherlands

Distributors for the United States and Canada:

ELSEVIER/NORTH-HOLLAND INC.
52, Vanderbilt Avenue
New York, N.Y. 10017

Library of Congress Cataloging in Publication Data
Main entry under title:

Guide dogs for the blind, their selection, development,
   and training.

   (Developments in animal and veterinary sciences ; 1)
   Includes index.
   1. Guide dogs. I. Pfaffenberger, Clarence J.
II. Series.
HV1780.S4G84   636.7'08'86   76-44518
ISBN 0-444-41520-3

Copyright © 1976 by Elsevier Scientific Publishing Company, Amsterdam

All rights reserved. No part of this publication may be reproduced, stored in a
retrieval system, or transmitted in any form or by any means, electronic,
mechanical, photocopying, recording, or otherwise, without the prior written
permission of the publisher,
Elsevier Scientific Publishing Company, Jan van Galenstraat 335, Amsterdam

Printed in The Netherlands

DEDICATION

To the memory of Clarence J. Pfaffenberger: gentleman,
scientist, and friend, who devoted much of his life and all of
his enthusiasm to the organization of canine services for the
blind.

126661

FOREWORD

In 1946 I received a letter from Clarence J. Pfaffenberger, representing the staff and officers of Guide Dogs for the Blind, Inc., located at San Rafael, California. As he explains in his history of the project, the operation was at that time a small and faltering one that was barely beginning to become effective. He wished to consult with me concerning the problem of selecting puppies that would later become suitable guides, and later met with me at the Jackson Laboratory. From this meeting we developed a long-time friendship and later set up a collaborative research project which included John L. Fuller and Benson E. Ginsburg, with the able assistance of Sherman Bielfelt.

Throughout the existence of the project we were treated with unfailing helpfulness and courtesy by the staff and officers of Guide Dogs for the Blind, Inc. The work that I did there was some of the most pleasant that I have ever accomplished, and the authors of this book hope that the results will not only be helpful in understanding and improving the work in San Rafael, but also provide an example of what can be done for other guide dog organizations that may be set up in the future.

Active data collection and analysis were carried on during the six years between 1961 - 67 and the book describes procedures as they were carried on at that time. Since then, the kennels, dormitories and training areas have been completely replaced by new and improved structures. Procedures for the selection and training of guide dogs are still carried on in much the same fashion with certain exceptions that will be noted in the appropriate places.

The use of guide dogs by blind people probably goes back for hundreds of years, but the first attempts to systematically train and provide dogs that would be widely available was set up in Switzerland under the leadership of Mrs. Dorothy Harrison Eustes at the location that became known as Fortunate Fields. Later, a similar institution was set up at Morristown, New Jersey, and became known as the Seeing Eye. This oldest and best known of such American institutions could serve only the East coast, and there was a demand for similar institutions elsewhere. Guide Dogs for the Blind, Inc. was organized to serve a similar function for the West coast. When this was done, Pfaffenberger and others found that the only scientific study of guide dogs was that done by Humphrey and Warner in 1934, and that it had only scratched the surface of the research problems that were involved. The trainers and other workers in San Rafael had to rely on their own knowledge and initiative to a large extent. Fortunately, under the leadership of Mr. Pfaffenberger, extensive and accurate records of the operation were kept, and these form the basis for the research reported here.

While the present volume by no means exhausts the possibilities for scientific research on guide dogs, it should provide a foundation of knowledge for anyone who undertakes a similar task in the future.

J. P. Scott
Bowling Green State University
Bowling Green, Ohio
December, 1975

Reference

Humphrey, E., and Warner, L. Working dogs: an attempt to produce a strain of German shepherds which combines working abilities with beauty of conformation. Baltimore, John Hopkins Press, 1934.

ACKNOWLEDGMENTS

The authors wish to acknowledge the unfailing help and co-operation of the research project staff including Mrs. Virginia Beauchamp, who made many of the photographs and did much of the typing, Mrs. Dorothy Carter, who prepared many of the drawings, and Mrs. Polly Redfield, research assistant. While not an official member of the research team, Mr. Fred Maynard, who had charge of the puppy placement program, contributed much time and energy to the project.

We also wish to thank the puppy testers who collected the data for this part of the project and particularly Mrs. Emma Belle Herak who directed their efforts. All these women contributed their time.

Finally, we wish to thank the entire staff of the Guide Dogs for the Blind, who have always been unfailingly helpful and courteous; Mrs. Shari Simon of Bowling Green University, who did the final typing of the manuscript for publication; and Mrs. Juanita Pfaffenberger, without whose help it could not have been completed.

Financial assistance during the data collecting phase of the project was provided by Grant Number NB-03336 from the National Institutes of Health.

CONTRIBUTORS

Clarence J. Pfaffenberger

Late vice-president, Guide Dogs for the Blind, Inc.
San Rafael, California, U.S.A.

John Paul Scott

Regent's Professor and
Director of Center for Research on Social Behavior
Bowling Green State University
Bowling Green, Ohio U.S.A.

John L. Fuller

Professor and Chairman, Department of Psychology
State University of New York at Binghamton
Binghamton, New York U.S.A.

Benson E. Ginsburg

Professor and Chairman
Department of Biobehavioral Sciences
University of Connecticut
Storrs, Connecticut

Sherman W. Bielfelt

Genetic Consultant
Guide Dogs for the Blind, Inc.
San Rafael, California

CONTENTS

HISTORY OF THE RESEARCH PROJECT

Clarence J. Pfaffenberger

Guide Dogs for the Blind, located in San Rafael, California, is a philanthropy supported by voluntary contributions and memberships. It chiefly serves the blinded people of the western part of the United States, but has no territorial limitations, and has supplied a number of dogs to blind people in Canada and even one in Mexico. It makes no charge for the dog and his equipment, for the board and room for four weeks while a student is in training nor for the education which the blind man or women receives concerning how to use the dog and care for it.

It is important to understand how this organization is set up and the historical reasons for it in order to appreciate both the successes achieved and the problems confronted by such an institution. In addition, the institution forms the background of the research described in this book. As will be seen, once organizational problems were overcome, the institution has been remarkably stable over the years.

Organizing the school. In early 1942 a group of prominent and public-spirited women working with the wounded service men at the U.S. Army Letterman Hospital asked the officers in charge, "What are you going to do with all these boys who have lost their sight? Has the government a program to supply them with guide dogs?"

They were informed that Seeing Eye at Morristown, New Jersey, would take as many as they could, but that no other provision had been made.

Feeling that this was an inadequate arrangement and that veterans from Western states should have a place where they could receive such aid closer to home, these women organized and incorporated Guide Dogs for the Blind for the purpose of

serving men and women blinded in the services. The articles
of incorporation wisely allowed others to benefit, but blinded
veterans of all wars have always been given priority.

In May 1942 the articles of incorporation were drawn and
executed, and the first officers and Board of Directors were
chosen. In the first publicity release announcing the opening
of the school by Guide Dogs for the Blind, Inc., the Los Gatos
Times, on Friday, August 21, 1942, made a prophecy that was to
ring true for the whole life of the developing institution,
"With all details of management complete and with their actual
training program underway, Guide Dogs for the Blind, Inc. is
now facing its biggest task: to obtain a steady supply of
dogs."

Obtaining a steady supply of ordinary dogs would have been
relatively easy, but procuring a supply of dogs that were suited for the work and capable of taking the responsibility for
leading the blind became such a serious problem during the following four years that it discouraged some of the Board members
who had set out so valiantly to serve the war veterans. Of
the original officers of the corporation, only three were serving when the school opened at San Rafael four and a half years
later, and not more than four or five of the other 35 founding
members were still actively participating. As to staff members, the problem of getting dogs trained and students graduated served more like a disposal device than a field of opportunity. Three business directors decided that this was not
the field for them. The fourth, Captain J. Stanley Head, who
had braved all kinds of danger heading the Canine Corps for
General McArthur from New Guinea to Japan and had returned a
war hero decorated with a silver star and a purple heart,
attempted the impossible task of living in Richmond (the only
place that could offer him housing) and commuting, first to
San Francisco to manage the office, then to Los Gatos to manage
the school, and then to San Rafael to superintend the building
of the kennels. He finally announced, "I would rather face
the enemy in the jungle than to continue facing him on the Bay
Bridge." He did stay on to get the dogs located and the puppy
testing program started at San Rafael, where Guide Dogs is now
established. The training program finally became stabilized

under the leadership of William F. Johns, who became Executive
Director of Guide Dogs for the Blind in 1949 and continued up
till his death in 1969. Himself an experienced dog breeder and
trainer, he was soon able to organize the training operation into a smooth-running and efficient process that has continued to
function well over the succeeding years.

Buildings and grounds.* The site is so secluded that road
maps are sent to prospective visitors, but its boundaries actually lie between freeway 101 to the east and Los Ranchitos Road,
the original highway 101, on the west. The entrance faces west,
and the school and campus of Guide Dogs for the Blind, Inc.,
occupy a beautifully landscaped half of the eleven acres owned
by this non-profit private philanthropic corporation.

Along the west border adjacent to Los Ranchitos Road a
five foot hedge shields the campus from the smoke, dust, and
sound of the passing traffic. The original plans for landscap-
ing were designed and donated by San Francisco's noted landscape
architect, Thomas D. Church. Many of the facilities here have
been donated or contributed by public spirited citizens. Clearly visible from the campus are the spire and dome of one of
Frank Lloyd Wright's last architectural achievements, the beautiful Marin County Court House.

The campus itself lies in the bowl of a beautiful valley
with high rolling hills on three sides, and along the sides of
these hills, climbing over their crests, have flowed the newer
residential areas of San Rafael and Terra Linda.

In March 1946, when the corporation purchased this land,
the picture was very different. Literally, it was pastoral.
All the surrounding higher land was used by large dairies as
pasture. So was the land where the school now stands, when
cows could get on it, but this land formed a natural basin
where the rain from all the surrounding high hills accumulated
and even the water from San Francisco Bay to the east surged
in at high tide under pressure of a storm. The only buildings

---

*These are described as they existed in 1966 prior to the con-
struction of the present enlarged and improved facilities on
the same grounds.

in sight were those of the dairy across Los Ranchitos Road from the school property.

This property was chosen by the Selection Committee of Guide Dogs for the Blind, Inc., after an exhaustive examination of those properties available in 1946 that would have been suitable for the school. The grounds had to be: large enough for expansion, situated where the training facilities for the students and their dogs could be properly conducted, located in an area where zoning would protect the organization from being subject to condemnation at some future date, and must be offered at a price that the young organization could afford. Properties for sale at distances of up to forty miles on all sides of San Francisco were considered.

The present location offered many advantages which seemed to outweigh the disadvantage of building on what was then a virtual swamp. They included: a promise from the county supervisors that the zoning would be such that there never need be fear of being condemned; a country road free of traffic upon which to train dogs and blind people to use their dogs (this is now one of the busy roads in the county leading to a multimillion dollar shopping district two blocks from the school); the proximity of San Rafael, which was then a residential town much on the order of a New England village, with many sleepy streets and lanes, some with sidewalks and curbs, some without; an ideal situation for starting the blind students in training with their dogs so that they would be adjusted to all these conditions when they went home; San Francisco only half an hour away across the Golden Gate Bridge. Thus, between San Rafael and San Francisco all types of traffic conditions were available for the training of the dogs and the instruction of the students. The famous Muir Woods were nearby to accustom students to taking their dogs into wooded and picnic areas and the Golden Gate Bridge was there to walk across. These two exercises have proven to be highlights in the experiences of the students during their month-long stay at Guide Dogs.

In the history of educational institutions, it is doubtful if one ever before began a campus by first building a dog breeding kennel, but this was done at San Rafael. Resident facilities were rented in a surplus army building, but a new kennel for the breeding stock was erected on the property. Additional kennels for the dogs in training were constructed, eventually followed by a school building which included a student residence area, dining room, kitchen and office.

Over the years other rooms were added to the school, while a separate building for office space and auditorium and additional residences and kennels have been added. As this is written (1976) the institution has completed a new building program providing expanded and improved facilities of all sorts.

The original puppy testing building used in this research, a memorial to Agnes Blank, who pioneered the record keeping of the puppy tests and pedigrees, was donated jointly by the San Francisco Dog Training Club and Mrs. Walter S. Heller. The San Francisco Dog Training Club also sent to Switzerland for the expensive measuring instruments. These have been in use ever since by the volunteer puppy testers, who had been trained and organized to take on the responsibility for six months before the new facilities were ready.

In February 1947 the new kennels were complete enough so that some dogs could be moved there from the original school located on a rented property at Los Gatos in the Santa Cruz Mountains, while the blind students with their dogs were moved to war surplus property near Mill Valley. As soon as the school buildings were complete, the entire operation was moved to San Rafael.

Breeding program. The reason that the school started with a breeding kennel and had its puppy testers trained and organized to start work as soon as the dogs could be moved to San Rafael was that, although two to four instructors trained a very large number of dogs during the first five years of the school's existence, less than 35 dogs all told had been well enough trained and adjusted to guide dog work to be considered safe to lead blind people.

People unacquainted with the great differences among dogs, even within the same breed, almost inevitably fail to comprehend the difficulties involved in producing dogs that have the necessary hereditary traits and also have experienced the proper environment to prepare them to take the responsibility of leading the blind. Overcoming these difficulties and setting up the present well-running organization required months and years of effort on the part of both executives and the training staff.

At the Dogs for Defense Regional Office in San Francisco, dogs were procured for all the U.S. armed services, for Seeing Eye at Morristown, New Jersey, and later for Guide Dogs for the Blind, Inc., during the three war years of 1942 through 1945. Mr. Clarence J. Pfaffenberger was Regional Director and Mrs. Walter S. Heller was a committee chairman of this office. After more than 6,000 dogs had been tested in order to find 1,800 dogs that could be used in the war effort, both of them became convinced that, in order to be successful for any purpose, dogs should be selected and bred for the certain definite qualities which would make them most useful for that particular job. A breeding program for War Dogs was set up under Mrs. Heller's charge. Later, those not used by the armed services were donated to Guide Dogs for the Blind, Inc.

Even while Guide Dogs was located at Los Gatos, a breeding program was started. The first litter of pups recorded on the Guide Dogs' Registry was born September 9, 1942.

Testing program. The School's Board of Directors, and especially the breeding committee, felt that it must not only raise its own dogs for training as guide dogs, but also that it must select and raise a very special group of breeding stock capable of producing puppies who would be suitable for guide dog work. With this in mind advice had been sought from the men thought best qualified to help, and classes had been set up in the Adult Schools of San Francisco to train a group of volunteer puppy testers to use whatever information that was then available and thought to be valuable in selecting both puppies and adult dogs. As a step toward a practical selection program, the school's instructors were asked to spell out as exactly as possible a description of the kind of dog they felt they needed.

In June, 1946, Mr. Clarence J. Pfaffenberger, a member of the Board of Directors, was invited to go east to meet at the

American Kennel Club office in New York with others selected
by the Club to draw up new rules and new types of exercises
for the Club's Obedience Trials. The Guide Dogs for the
Blind's Board of Directors asked Mr. Pfaffenberger to take
some extra time while in the east to learn what was known
about testing puppies so as to determine the inherited traits
for guide and breeding stock.

After he had made calls on five persons, each of whom had
some knowledge of this sort of study, Dr. J. Paul Scott at the
Jackson Laboratory in Bar Harbor, Maine, was suggested as the
man who was then doing most in the study of dog behavior. Mr.
Pfaffenberger made an appointment to meet Dr. Scott in Bar
Harbor. Here he gathered not only such information as he could
but enlisted Dr. Scott and, soon after, Edna DuBuis and Drs.
John L. Fuller and Clarence C. Little, as advisors in the project. They were all helpful in setting up the puppy testing
program.

In June 1946 Dr. Scott helped Mr. Pfaffenberger plan a set
of tests to give to guide dog puppies. Guide dog puppies were
first tested by these tests in February, 1947, and a somewhat
revised and improved version of them has been used ever since.

History of the 4-H program for cooperative puppy-rearing.
The 4-H is a youth organization sponsored by the United States
Department of Agriculture through the Agricultural Extension
Service in each state. It functions through volunteer leaders
who organize local clubs including boys and girls from ages 9
through 19. Formerly a purely rural activity, it has spread
to towns and cities. The name--4-H--stands for "Head, Heart,
Hands and Health," and the activities of each club are center-
ed around individual projects, usually designed to be exhibited at State Fairs. One such project now done in many states,
besides California, is the rearing of a puppy destined to be a
guide dog.

Like so many of the other constructive developments at
Guide Dogs for the Blind, Inc., the 4-H program was started by
Mrs. Walter S. Heller, then vice president of Guide Dogs, who
in September 1946 persuaded the very doubtful directors of the
University of California Agriculture Extension Service to in-

clude the guide dog puppy raising program as a full-fledged
4-H project in California. The project was initiated in Octo-
ber, and puppies started arriving in 4-H Club member's homes,
mostly delivered by Mrs. Heller in her own car.

That the 4-H guide dog puppy raising program had been in
actual operation on a rather large scale 16 months before any
puppy tests were given is important to note, since this means
that dogs given the puppy testing always went through the same
intermediate training before being trained as guide dogs.

It is also worth noting that the 4-H program was popular
from the start. Two of the main doubts felt by the directors
of the 4-H program were: 1) That to give up a puppy after all
the trouble of raising and training, just when the job was done
and his companionship was at its best seemed too much to ask of
any youngster, and 2) that to ask a child and his family to
spend considerable money raising a guide dog when he could at
the same time invest an equal amount or less into something
like a steer which would make him some money, not only seemed
like asking too much of a child, but contrary to all the plans
which had been set up to make an independent business-like person of each club member.

There was a considerable change of feeling about the project as soon as it was seen how well it was received, and a
statement on August 1, 1958 seems to well express the feeling
of rapport which now exists between 4-H Clubs in California and
the Guide Dogs for the Blind.

"4-H members in 34 California counties have raised 153
guide dog puppies during the last 12 months," announced Mr. R.
O. Monosmith, state 4-H Club leader. "There are also 14 Club
members who are caring for Guide Dogs studs and bitches as a
regular 4-H project. Of the many projects available to the 4-H
Club member, the guide dog program is the richest in terms of
value to the youngster's development."

Many a parent has joined in this sentiment in writing and
in personal reports to Guide Dogs. Typical is one letter which
says, "No other project of any kind which my child has ever
undertaken has done so much good for him in developing his attitude toward life itself and his attitude toward his fellow
man."

This enthusiasm was present from the beginning and kept the program going through the difficult early times of organization. At one time there were twice as many 4-H children who wanted puppies as there were puppies available. In addition there was no regular schedule set up either among the Farm Advisors who had charge in the counties, or the breeding committee at Guide Dogs, which kept the Farm Advisor informed of the possible production at Guide Dogs, or one which kept Guide Dogs informed of the number of 4-H children who would be willing to raise puppies in any one year. Another element of early confusion was the fact that whereas most 4-H programs were organized on a yearly basis, starting about when school opened in the fall and ending after the summer fairs, the Guide Dog program had to run continually, requiring 12 different groups of dogs starting training at regular one-month intervals.

A more serious blow came in 1949 and 50, when Guide Dogs decided to stop accepting over-large dogs for training. Both a faulty breeding program and the decision to castrate dogs before sending them to the 4-H homes had led to producing many dogs that were too large to be used as guide dogs. The reaction to this decision pointed up the need for better communication between Guide Dogs and the 4-H puppy raisers. The children, instead of being pleased at being allowed to keep their pets, felt that their training and care for a particular goal were being wasted through no fault of their own. Enthusiasm dropped sharply, and so few requests for puppies were made that a public appeal for other homes had to be broadcast. Although all the puppies were placed in some home or other, the results proved very disappointing compared to those achieved by 4-H puppy raisers.

As a result of this experience, the Research Committee of Guide Dogs in 1954 asked Mr. Pfaffenberger, who had recently retired from the San Francisco School Department, to make a three-month study of the problem with the object of setting up an improved program of cooperation between all groups. In April, 1955, the minutes of the Board of Directors show that his report met with the Board's approval and that a budget of $200.00 a month expense money plus transportation was approved. At the end of the first three months Mr. and Mrs. Pfaffenberger had traveled 3,509 miles in their own car, had made 85 calls at prospective homes and the county farm advisors' offices, and had delivered six puppies.

Every phase of activity at Guide Dogs for the Blind, Inc.-- breeding, selection, testing, training and supply program--was made more suitable for meaningful research by this new arrangement, because there now was in the making the most uniform set of breeding, selecting and rearing controls that Guide Dogs had ever had.

In each community where puppies were to be reared, the people who were known as good obedience, field-trial or dog-show people were consulted, and in each county when a 4-H program was renewed, someone from this group of local dog people took up the task of helping the Farm Advisors. This had been done back in 1945 through 1950, but had almost been forgotten by 1955. These liaison representatives not only organized the weekly training schools for puppies and puppy raisers, but visited each new prospective home to explain the program and the special problems involved. In addition, puppies were no longer sent to their new homes by express, but delivered personally by a Guide Dog representative, who also visited with the family and supervised the important first contacts between puppy and family.

There was a lot of enthusiasm for the project, and it was developed county by county as fast as puppies could be bred from those of the Guide Dogs breeding stock who were known to have produced good litters. New breeding stock, particularly of the golden retriever breed, was introduced from dogs and bitches who performed well in obedience and field trials. Several litters of Chesapeake Bay retrievers and Labradors from breedings of dogs successful in field trials and hunting were also tried with good success. Since 1955 the 4-H program has had no more set-backs and has grown and expanded on the sound basis set up for it, until it is now an essential and valuable part of the Guide Dogs organization.

History of the research project. In 1960 both the Board of Directors of Guide Dogs for the Blind, Inc., and the scientists who had become interested in helping with the development of the puppy program at San Rafael since 1946, felt that all the data which had been carefully assembled concerning the developments of this program would offer useful analytical material both for practical use at Guide Dogs and for use by scientists interested in animal behavior, heredity, environmental influences, and the ability of man to improve desirable traits by careful selection and development of individuals.

A proposal was made to the Department of Health, Education and Welfare for a grant to make such a study. The scientists included in the proposal were the three who had helped for years on a volunteer basis: Drs. J. Paul Scott, John L. Fuller and Benson E. Ginsburg. The late Dr. T. J. Hage, Associate Professor at the University of California at Davis, joined later and did an extensive hip subluxation study which he had not quite completed at the time of his death in November of 1966.

On June 1, 1961, the grant, having been approved, became effective, and more and more of Mr. Pfaffenberger's time was required as its principal investigator. A part-time staff consisting of a secretary-photographer, Mrs. Nathan Beauchamp; a mathematician-medical artist, Mrs. William Carter; a researcher of social service records, Mrs. William Redfield, was set up, while a full time geneticist and computer programmer, Sherman Bielfelt, began investigating the mass of data which had accumulated since the school began in 1942.

In November, 1962, the Pfaffenbergers gave up almost all management of the puppy placement program, and Mr. Fred Maynard who had been assisting for more than a year, took charge of this part of the guide dog work. The grant was awarded for 5 years, but permission was given in 1966 to continue through the sixth year without additional funds. During the summer of 1966, twenty years after the original plan for testing was born, the authors of this book, together with the late Dr. T. J. Hage, met to plan the final data analysis and the writing and editing of the volume at Guide Dogs for the Blind, Inc., in San Rafael, California. This book is the result.

EARLY REARING AND TESTING

Clarence J. Pfaffenberger and J. P. Scott

Natural Developmental Periods In The Dog

During the early days when the program of puppy testing was being developed at Guide Dogs for the Blind, workers at the Jackson Laboratory in Bar Harbor were making an intensive observational and experimental study of the normal development of behavior in several breeds of dogs. Based on this information, it is possible to predict with considerable accuracy what a puppy can do at any given age and thus decide on an appropriate scheme of care and training (Scott and Fuller, 1965).

The behavioral development of the dog may be divided into several periods, based on important changes in social relationships. Each period is characterized by a major behavioral process. During the Neonatal Period, lasting from birth until approximately 2 weeks of age, the puppy is both blind and deaf, and its behavior is almost entirely concerned with the process of neonatal nutrition, which is accomplished by nursing. During this period the puppy is ordinarily well insulated against damage from psychological sources, both by its own immaturity and by the care of the mother.

During the Transition Period, which takes place between 2 and 3 weeks of age, the behavior of the puppy is transformed from patterns concerned with neonatal life to those of an adult. At approximately 13 days, the eyes are fully open, and by the end of the following week the ears are also open and the puppy begins to hear. He walks instead of crawls; the teeth erupt, and he begins to lap semi-solid food. Beginning at approximately 3 weeks of age, the puppy can be readily conditioned, i.e., important new capacities for learning have been developed. At the same time, new patterns of social behavior begin to appear--playful fighting and tail wagging.

The Period of Socialization begins at 3 weeks. During this time the puppy will rapidly and easily form emotional attachments, both to people and to other dogs. The process can take place with a relatively small amount of contact; a reasonably normal relationship can develop with no more than two 20 minute periods of contact per week (Fuller, 1967). The peak of this capacity occurs between 6 and 8 weeks of age and declines thereafter. If socialization does not take place by 12 weeks of age, the process becomes increasingly difficult and can never be really satisfactorily achieved afterward. When puppies were raised in a 1-acre field surrounded by a high board fence, so that they could neither see nor come into contact with people, they acted like little wild animals at 14 weeks of age (Freedman, King, and Elliot, 1961). Using confinement and hand feeding, they could be partially tamed, but they were always shy and timid compared to puppies that had extensive human contact at the earlier ages.

Final weaning also takes place during the period of socialization. Food other than milk is first taken shortly after 3 weeks, and most bitches stop nursing their pups between 7 and 10 weeks. The end of the period can be placed at about 12 weeks, the time when puppies begin to make voluntary excursions away from their nest or den area.

During the Juvenile Period which follows, the most important processes are the maturation of physique and motor skills. This period extends up to the age of sexual maturity, which may occur as early as 5 months, or as much as a year later, depending on the breed and individual. If permitted, bitches will usually mate during their first estrus cycles. Thus the Pubertal Period, in which an animal is sexually mature but has still not produced offspring, is often quite short and soon followed by the birth of the young and the onset of the Parental Period.

Physical growth is approximately two-thirds completed by the age of 4 months and continues at a gradually decreasing rate until well into the second year. On the average, males grow faster than females at all ages, and the size differences become more and more pronounced after 4 months (Scott & Fuller, 1965).

Relationship between the testing program and natural periods of development. The puppy testing program begins during the height of the process of socialization, at 8 weeks of age, and continues through to the end of the socialization period at 12 weeks.* It therefore serves a function beyond that of screening the puppies, that of providing the basis of socialization to human beings through contacts with the testers.

Should this socialization be performed at the kennels or in the home? The guide dog will live its life in two important places, the kennel and training school, and the home of the blind person. Preparation for the first is provided by the puppy socialization and testing program, and the period in a 4-H club member's home provides the second. Experience indicates that the home environment contact can not be delayed long beyond 12 weeks of age (Pfaffenberger and Scott, 1959) without impairing performance as a guide dog.

In general, a dog must be introduced to the scene of its adult life before 3 months of age in order to permit successful adjustment as an adult. Dogs left in a kennel beyond this time usually become permanently shy and often make very unsatisfactory pets (Scott and Fuller, 1965; Krushinski, 1962).

No good experimental data exist on the results of placing the puppies directly in homes at 6 to 8 weeks of age, but results with 2 litters were poor. The results with dogs from other sources reared in private homes and donated for guide dog training as adults have usually been less satisfactory than those with dogs reared under the program here described. The difficulty with home rearing alone is that of providing the pups with the necessary additional early experience under kennel and training conditions. A home-reared dog would need to be given training experience in the kennel before 12 weeks of age, and this would be difficult to arrange from a practical viewpoint.

Summarizing our current information about dog development, we can say that the period from 3 to 12 weeks of age is a crit-

---

*At present (1976), the program begins at 6 weeks and extends through 10 weeks, thus overlapping the peak period of socialization.

ical one, both for the formation of primary social relationships
with dogs and people, and for the introduction of the puppy to
its future work and physical environment (Scott, Stewart and
DeGhett, 1974). The puppy needs to be socialized to a variety
of people so that it will be able to change from home owner to
trainer and then to a blind person without being emotionally
upset. It needs to be introduced to streets and buildings similar to those through which it will eventually lead a blind person. It also needs to be introduced to the two principal environments in which it will live: the kennel and training quart-
ers, and a home. In its eventual life as a guide dog it will
combine the results of all these kinds of experience in one existence.

These conclusions are based on both theoretical and practical evidence and lead to a method of rearing which emphasizes
human contact and a wide experience with physical objects.
When it is considered that the puppies are raised from 12 weeks
to approximately 12 months of age in 4-H homes in 5 states, and
then returned to San Rafael to be trained by the instructors,
who take them out each day on the streets of San Rafael and San
Francisco, and when it is also considered that the breeding females are brought in from individual homes and kenneled near
each other to whelp and nurse their litters, the difference
from the isolated kennels of laboratories and universities, or
even from the average dog breeder's kennel, is marked. Added
to this is the taking of the 12 week old puppies to class once
a week to be trained by the 4-H child and to mix with other puppies. The children even take the puppies in stores and on public transportation. Also, there are visitors who walk freely
about the grounds at San Rafael, looking at any of the dogs in
the kennels and even the puppies seven weeks of age or older,
as they come out into the runs.

This exposure of the guide dog population, so different
from the carefully guarded dogs and puppies of most breeders,
largely came about because of an experiment that was performed
by accident. Soon after the 4-H program was initiated, it became evident that dogs from 4-H homes were so superior that
every effort was made to place the puppies in these homes. But
the early reluctance of some 4-H clubs to take the puppies pro-

duced a back-log at Guide Dogs. Because of this, some puppies remained in the kennels various lengths of time; in a few cases up to 9 months of age. While these happenings proved to be disadvantageous for the puppies concerned, they supplied material for verifying a number of important things about the best way to bring up a puppy to become a really good guide dog.

Like many other disappointments, this one turned out to be a lead to an important discovery, one which helped to solve the problem of having so many excellent dogs fail because they refused to take the responsibility of making a decision for a blind master. Such decisions occur when the dog is confronted with a problem that his master could not possibly solve, such as a new obstruction across the sidewalk along which they have passed every day; an obstruction which actually blocks the entire street such as a ditch dug across from wall to wall; situations where the crossing of a street seems perfectly safe to the master but the dog can see a car speeding down upon them; or where there is a low awning or tree limb, or an open manhole. In these cases the dog must make his own decision and refuse to obey any command which will endanger him and his master.

For years, not only Guide Dogs but all other schools training dogs for the blind found that many dogs will refuse to take this responsibility for independent decisions. The worst of it is that such dogs have often shown the greatest promise. They have trained well and shown no sign of this fault until they have to lead a trainer under blindfold. Some do not show the fault until they actually have to lead their blind masters or mistresses. This, then, means a great disappointment to the trainer as well as a loss of investment in time and money in a dog who cannot be trusted and, therefore, must be rejected.

From the beginning of the testing program, this had been one of the problems that had been studied, and no test had been evolved which showed any promise of discriminating in advance between those dogs that would accept responsibility and those which would not. Every person who might be able to suggest an answer to whom Guide Dogs could appeal had been sought out. The problem at last caused Pfaffenberger to apply for a John Simon Guggenheim Memorial Foundation Fellowship so that he could take all of the testing records to Bar Harbor to study them under the sponsorship of Scott, who had collaborated with him in setting up the puppy tests in 1946. He obtained a Fellowship for 1953-54 and a later extension for the following year.

At Bar Harbor Pfaffenberger examined the records with respect to everything that had been recorded about the life and experience of all the dogs who refused to take responsibility. What things did these dogs have in common? In their common experience was there anything that could be interpreted as being the evil that robbed them of self confidence and courage to do something right, against their master's command?

The answer came through very clearly. "Too long a time spent in the kennels after puppy testing stopped at 12 weeks." This effect was evident in both those puppies which had passed the test and those that had failed. Ordinarily, only those puppies who have passed the puppy tests are placed in the 4-H homes, but controls are necessary at times to evaluate the reliability of the puppy tests and also the selected breeding stock.

In order that a control group might be included in the analysis of the effect of the prolonged stay in the kennels upon the behavior of adult dogs, a population of 154 dogs was selected. This was taken as a block from a continuous production. The entire block had been 188 puppies. Of these there were records completed on only 154, the rest having been lost through various accidents of death and disease. Of the 154, one hundred and twenty four had passed the puppy tests and thirty had failed. The thirty were the controls. All were raised by the same system, and only Pfaffenberger knew which were the controls. Thus, there could not have been any prejudgments made because of their puppy scores.

The results are given in Table 2.1. In those puppies which passed the tests, 90% of the dogs removed at 12 weeks became guides, while only 30% succeeded if kept in the kennels 3 or more weeks longer. Of the dogs that failed the puppy tests, none succeeded as guides if kept in the kennels beyond that same period. Statistically, these results are highly significant ($p < .01$, chi square) with respect to the time the pups left the kennel.

At the time this study was made (Pfaffenberger and Scott,

Table 2.1

RESULTS OF RETAINING PUPPIES IN KENNELS BEYOND 12 WEEKS

Number of Puppies Placed In 4-H Homes After Completion of Tests at 12 Weeks	Became Guides		Failed In Training	
	Number	Percent	Number	Percent
(124 Puppies that passed test)				
40 within one week	36	90	4	10
22 within 2 weeks	19	86	3	14
19 within 3 weeks	11	58	8	42
43 after 3 weeks	13	30	30	70
Total	79	64	45	36
(30 Puppies selected as controls from the 64 that had failed the puppy test)				
6 within one week	1	17	5	83
2 within 2 weeks	0	0	2	100
9 within 3 weeks	4	44	5	56
13 after 3 weeks	0	0	13	100
Total	5	16	25	84

1959) there was no clearcut evidence as to why the dogs were affected by this experience, but it is now clear that these animals were suffering from the "kennel dog syndrome" (Scott, 1970), which seems to result chiefly from emotional shock when an older animal is removed from a simple familiar environment into a strange and complex one. A more drastic effect, the "isolation syndrome", results from rearing a puppy in the more restricted environment of a small kennel in which the puppy is visually isolated from the rest of the world (Fuller, 1967; Fuller and Clark, 1966a, 1966b).

Conclusion. Puppies undergo an emotional shock when removed from a familiar environment at any age from 3 weeks onward, but at the earlier ages recover much more rapidly and
show no ill aftereffects. Likewise, the emotional shock is
much lessened if the transition to the new environment is made
gradually and by degrees rather than suddenly and all at once.
Seen in this light, the puppy testing and training program con-
formed in almost an ideal way to the natural periods of development that were determined by experiments at the Jackson Laboratory and experience at Guide Dogs for the Blind (Figure 2.1).
The puppy testing and training program (for it was indeed a
training program as well) began at 6 weeks of age with taking
the puppy out of the kennel individually for short periods of
contact with strange people and also with the strange environment outside the kennel. The times were not long enough so
that the puppy became alarmed, and the contacts with people
were made pleasant. Beginning at 8 weeks and extending through
12 the puppies were put through the weekly testing program, involving exposure to a large number of people and to a simulated
street environment including many of the unexpected incidents
and hazards to which an adult guide dog must become accustomed.
At 12 weeks the puppies were transferred to the 4-H homes, this
being the latest age at which a puppy can be satisfactorily
introduced into a new environment. For a completely kennel-
reared puppy this might almost be too late, but the guide dog
puppies were prepared for at least some aspects of the outside
world by their weekly testing and training sessions. Thus the
early training of the puppies was consistent with the general
rule that a puppy must be introduced to its future environment
and life work at least before the age of 12 weeks and preferably
from 6 weeks onward.

Life History of a Guide Dog. This is described as it was
done during the time when this data was collected. Breeding
stock was maintained in the homes of volunteer workers. When a
bitch came into estrus, she was taken into the kennels for mating, and thereafter returned to the volunteer home until 5 days
before she was due to whelp, when she was brought to the kennels again for the birth of the puppies.

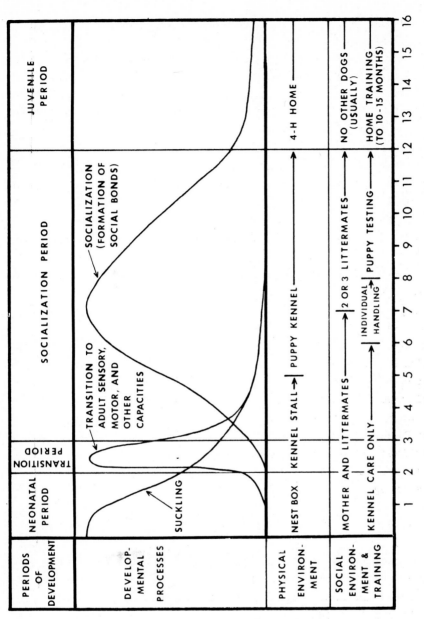

Figure 2.1. The puppy rearing program in relation to natural periods of development.

Mother and litter were kept in the nursery as a unit until the puppies were 5 weeks of age. For these 5 weeks, the puppies were raised under the following system. All mothers were housed in separate stalls in the radiant heated nursery. Each stall had a whelping box 85cm X 125cm in area with sides 20-25cm high. This box was raised enough off the floor to prevent moisture from accumulating. As the puppies were born each puppy was carefully examined and placed on an electric pad in a separate box to keep it warm while the other puppies were being whelped. When the bitch had finished whelping, she was given the puppies, and care was taken to see that each puppy got its stomach full and nursed successfully during the first hour it was with its mother. Each mother and her puppies had their own enclosed stall in the kennel, and the whelping box served to keep the puppies close to their mother for the first 2 weeks. The mother was always free to exercise in her own chainlink fenced, concrete floored, outside run, 1.5m wide and 6.0m long.

At about 2 weeks of age the whelping box was removed so that the litter had the freedom of the 1.2 X 1.5m radiant heated stall. At 4 weeks of age pablum and milk were given as supplementary feeding. Meal and meat were gradually added as the puppies were able to eat more solid food.

At 5 weeks of age the mother and puppies were moved to a puppy kennel that was much like the nursery but larger. Here they lived until they were 12 weeks of age. The mother and all her litter stayed together until the puppies were weaned at 7 weeks of age, when they were placed in smaller groups of 3 and 4 in each kennel run.

At 6 weeks of age socialization with people was begun. One of the puppy testers who specialized in socialization took each puppy, one at a time, entirely away from its mother and litter mates to some place where it could be played with on the lawn for 5 minutes. Each puppy in the litter was taken in turn for his own individual socialization. This was repeated with every puppy at 7 weeks of age. Thus each puppy was individually given a brief experience in a strange place in company with a strange handler, circumstances which promote the formation of a social bond. These two socialization exercises, a week apart, were given on Thursdays, as this was the day on which all puppy tests were given. The day was originally selected for the convenience of the 30 volunteer puppy testers.

At 8 weeks of age the puppies were given their first tests. Each puppy spent 20 to 30 minutes taking a series of tests. On each Thursday of the following 4 weeks, similar but progressive tests were given. Following the 12th week test, the puppies were placed individually in homes where they were cared for by 4-H club members. At approximately one year of age (but actually varying from 10 to 15 months) the grown puppies were returned to the kennels, where their formal training was begun. Performance during the training period was, of course, the ultimate criterion of success. If the young dog responded properly to training it became a guide dog. After varying periods of training, the trainers might decide that the dog could not be successfully trained. In this case the dog was returned to the 4-H puppy raiser, if desired, for a personal pet.

The Testing Program

As we have seen earlier, the first results of setting up a training program at Guide Dogs for the Blind in 1942 were very poor, despite the fact that good training methods were being used. In 1946 it was decided to institute a supervised breeding, puppy testing, and puppy raising program, so that the dog's development could be followed from birth until one year of age when the actual training was begun.

Since there was such a high rate of failures, a screening test was set up to weed out those puppies which had a high probability of failure, so that time and money would not be wasted on their rearing and training. Experience with human aptitude tests, especially those dealing with motor performance, had indicated that the best predictability of behavior was achieved by tests which most closely simulate the future performance required (Anastasi, 1961). Therefore, Pfaffenberger designed a test for young puppies which would mimic as far as possible the conditions under which the animals would later be trained as guides. This test and the general results obtained from it are described below (Tables 2.2-2.7).

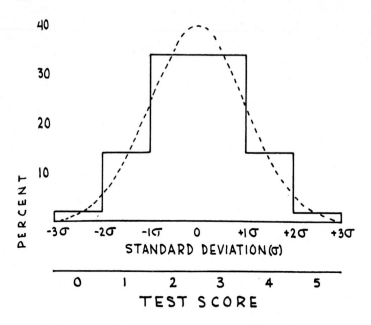

Figure 2.2. Ideal normal curve (dotted line) and test score distribution (solid line).

Scoring. All tests were scored on a 6 point scale ranging from 0 to 5. If the distribution of scores were symmetrical and normal it should follow the curve shown in Figure 2.2, with a mean (or average) of 2.5, a standard deviation of 1.0, and a range extending to 3 times the standard deviation in either direction. Such a score, though limited, is therefore adequate for applying almost any statistical technique based on a normal distribution.

As will be seen in Chapter 3, the scores given to the puppies usually ran somewhat higher than the ideal average, and the standard deviation was somewhat smaller than 1.0 (Figure 2.3). Part of this reduction in variation resulted from reduction imposed by the upper limit of the scale, and part from the system of scoring itself. The final scores were computed from averages and, as a general rule, the fractions on any average score were dropped. The result was, of course, to discard part of the variance.

The number of assigned scores varied according to the test. In every case but the Heel test scores were made by at

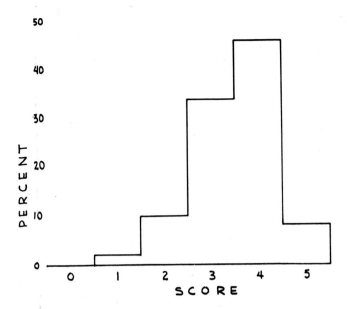

Figure 2.3.   Distribution of Sit scores for 187 German shepherd
               puppies tested from 1953-1955. Note that the
               curve, while roughly normal in shape, is skewed
               to the right, indicating that the testers ranked
               most of the puppies as superior.

least two people and the results averaged. In the case of the
Sit, Come, and Fetch scores, each performance was rated by two
people and the final score was the average of the two scores
given on the final week, representing presumably the best performance of the animal.

    The Trained Response and Willing-in-Training scores were
obtained from the same tests, but the final scores were the average of all scores given from 8 to 11 weeks of age. Each
score had a positive and negative version consisting of 8 questions scored separately by different people. The final score
was the average of the 64 scores so obtained, again with the
fractions eliminated.

    A similar scoring system was used for the Body Sensitivity
and Ear Sensitivity tests, and the final score was obtained in
the same way. There were 5 scores given on a Simulated Traffic
test administered at 12 weeks of age. Under ideal conditions,
this test was rated by 8 different people, resulting in a group

126661

of 40 scores. Similarly 16 scores were given for Footing-Crossing and 24 for the Closeness test. The results were averaged and the fractions dropped. The Heel score was based on individual ratings made by the tester herself; the final score was the average of the last two scores with the fraction eliminated.

All of the scores were therefore mean scores, but based on very different total numbers, ranging from 2 in the Sit, Come, and Heel scores to 64 in some of the others. Since estimates of both the mean and variance are more accurate with larger numbers, differences in these latter tests are likely to be more meaningful.

Personnel. The Heel test required only one person who acted as both tester and scorer for each dog. All of the other tests used one person who only handled the dog, sometimes being assisted by other individuals who administered stimuli, and always by others who acted as scorers. With the exception of the Heel and Simulated Traffic tests, there were two scorers for each test. As stated above, the latter test employed 8 scorers, although this number was sometimes reduced if not enough people were present.

All scores were made independently, but every effort was made to ensure agreement by the use of specific directions. Ratings by two scorers rarely differed by more than one point. The same persons acted as testers and scorers for all tests of the same litter, and there were very few changes in personnel over the period of years in which the data analyzed in this book were collected.

Group I training tests. The testing area was a room approximately 3 x 6 meters in size, at one end of which was a raised desk behind which the scorers sat quietly. The puppy could see only their heads and the tops of their bodies. After leading the dog into the area the tester knelt or squatted beside the puppy, and called out its name and the command "Sit!". At the same time she jacknifed the puppy into a sitting position by using her right hand to press backward on the puppy's chest and her left hand to press forward on the rear of the puppy's stifle joint. As soon as the puppy would sit, the tester

Table 2.2

SCHEDULE OF TESTING
(All tests given on Thursdays)

Name of Test	Age in Weeks						
	6	7	8	9	10	11	12
Preliminary Socialization	X	X					
Weight: check sense organs, teeth; measure shoulder height			X	X	X	X	X
Group I							
Sit			X	X	X	X	X
Come			X	X	X	X	X
Fetch			X	X	X	X	X
Trained Response			X	X	X	X	
Willing-in-Training			X	X	X	X	
Group II							
Body Sensitivity			X	X	X	X	
Ear Sensitivity			X	X	X	X	
New Experience Response			X	X	X	X	
Willing-New-Experience			X	X	X	X	
Group III							
Traffic							X
Footing-Crossing							X
Closeness (reaction to obstructions)							X
Heel			X	X	X	X	X

would hold her right hand over its head in the "hand-sit" signal. This exercise was repeated three times, and was scored as the Sit Test.

The Come Test was given in the following way. The tester moved as far away as possible from the puppy, knelt or squatted and called the puppy while clapping her hands: "(name of puppy) Come!". The call was repeated up to 5 times if necessary. A perfect score was given if the puppy came immediately after being called once.

The puppy was then given training in retrieving a rubber ball, the results being scored as the Fetch Test. The tester called the puppy, showed it the ball, and tried to get it excited before throwing the ball several feet away. As she threw the ball she called: "(name of puppy) Fetch!" in a lively and encouraging tone of voice, and continued clapping her hands and encouraging the puppy. No attempt was made to force the puppy to retrieve, and no discouragement was given. This is playful retrieving, a type of retrieving which permits considerable freedom to the animal. As a guide dog, the animal would later be trained in forced retrieving as part of the services performed for a blind person. This test was given 3 times at 8 weeks, 4 at 9 weeks, 5 at 10 weeks, 4 at 11 weeks and 3 at 12 weeks. The normal puppy was expected to learn all three of these exercises in 5 lessons.

As well as scoring for performance on these three tests, the scorers filled out two other forms answering questions about the puppy's behavior. The Willing-in-Training score included the 8 statements in Table 2.3 listed in positive and negative form, one scorer grading the positive statements and another the negative ones in the usual 6 point scale. These statements reflected whether or not the puppy was fearful or at ease, afraid to move or moved freely, was indifferent or friendly to the tester, was unresponsive or responsive to encouragement, urinated or was continent, was upset by the new situation or was confident, and was obstinate or willing in its responses. As will be seen from the nature of the items, 7 of the 8 statements were concerned with fearfulness and only one with willingness, with the result that the score might better be called Confidence-Timidity rather than Willing-in-Training.

RIGHT--Mrs. Emma Belle
Herak administers
the Fetch test,
while two scorers
observe from a
bench above the
arena.

LEFT--Puppy in
arena used for
Group II
tests, being
tested for its
response to a
strange person
at 8 weeks.
The puppy
gives a good
response--
interest, with
no sign of
fear.

LEFT--Heel test
(Group III).
Note that the pup-
py is being
trained to walk
on the left and
slightly in front
of the person--
the same position
required of an
adult guide dog.

RIGHT--Simulated
traffic
test (Group
III). The
puppy reacts
fearfully
to a cart
suddenly
rolled up
behind it.

Table 2.3

ITEMS IN WILLING TEMPERAMENT
AND WILLING-NEW-EXPERIENCE SCORES

Positive Statements	Negative Statements
1. Puppy seems at ease in pen; or if not in pen, at ease on leash	Nervous in new situation Vocalizes a lot; some; none
2. Moves about in puppy pen freely; or if on leash does not struggle	Refuses to move from where it is placed
3. Looks pen and tester over calmly; or looks situation over calmly on leash	Indifferent to new situation and people
4. Friendly with testers	Unfriendly toward testers
5. Responds to tester's encouragement	Undependable in responses. Acts one way one time and another way at another time to similar situations
6. Does not urinate from fear	Urinates from fear
7. Is not upset by strange people and things	Shows that strange people and things upset it
8. Is willing to do what tester wants it to do and shows pleasure in doing it	Obstinate and refuses to do what tester wishes

The other score given at the same time and based on the same behavior was called the Trained Response score. The statements seen in Table 2.4 are again set in positive and negative form[*], each answered by a different scorer. These items chiefly involved specific reactions to the tester and the environment, i.e., whether the puppy was afraid of the tester or not, was over-excited or cooperated calmly, did or did not pay atten-

---

[*]At the present time (1976), the scoring procedures illustrated in Tables 2.3 and 2.4 are being used in a simplified form, particularly by the elimination of the negative scale.

Table 2.4

ITEMS IN TRAINED RESPONSE
AND NEW-EXPERIENCE-RESPONSE SCORES

Positive Statements	Negative Statements
1. Adjusts to tester readily	Afraid of tester
2. Cooperates well with tester	Is "tester happy"
3. Follows moving objects with eyes	Does not follow moving objects with eyes
4. Adjusts to new environment readily	Does not adjust to new environment readily
5. Shows curiosity about unfamiliar objects and people	Does not show curiosity about unfamiliar objects and people
6. Seems to remember previous experience	Does not seem to remember previous experience
7. Seems to try to do what tester wants	Does not try to do what tester wants
8. Persists in solving problem	Has no persistence in solving problem

tion to moving objects, adjusted slowly or readily to the new
environment, showed no curiosity or was curious about new objects and people, did or did not remember previous experience,
tried to do what the tester wanted or not, and showed persis-
tence or not in performing a task. The nature of the items
overlaps somewhat with those in the other form, and the Willing-
in-Training and the Trained Response score were originally designed as an attempt to estimate the intelligence of the animal.
Actually they gave a picture of an animal that was calm but curious, alert and cooperative, or the reverse. Many of these
qualities are emotional in themselves, and they are most likely
to be disturbed by the appearance of fearful behavior. This
score should therefore be highly correlated with that of Willing-in-Training, but be somewhat less precise because of the
nature of the questions.

Table 2.5

NOVEL STIMULI USED IN NEW EXPERIENCE TEST

8 Weeks

   Strange person
   Flashlight
   Sound of police whistle
   Pinch between toes (slight
     pain)

9 Weeks

   4 strange persons at once
   White sheet of paper
   Door chime
   Pinch ear

10 Weeks

   Tester pets puppy
   Drags leash leather on
     pen bottom
   Sound of palm buzzer
   Command of "Down"

11 Weeks (on leash)

   Command of "Come"
   Auto horn
   Handles tail
   Stranger suddenly jumps
     toward puppy, stamping
     feet

Tests in Group II: responses to novel stimuli. After the
puppies were through with the training test they were led into
an area just outside the building and given a series of tests
which measured the puppy's reactions to novel stimuli. These
stimuli were of course changed from week to week and are listed
in Table 2.5. They involved reactions to strange people, objects, and sounds, as well as to various sorts of mildly painful stimuli. No attempt was made to severely frighten the puppy, and it should ideally have responded with a momentary alerting or startle reaction and then adjusted rapidly. The score
sheets were based on 2 series of 8 positive and negative statements, one set chiefly relating to pain (Body Sensitivity), and
the other to reactions to strange noises (Ear Sensitivity).
These items are given in Tables 2.6 and 2.7. The scorers also
filled out scores for the same items which were scored in the
Trained Response and Willing-in-Training scores, but here applied to the different tests in Group II. These scores were
called New Experience Response and Willing in New Experience.
Again, these scores were related to emotional reactions, but
this time in reaction to novel stimuli rather than to training.
In those scores in which the same score sheets were used in
Group I and Group II tests, it would be expected that the

Table 2.6

ITEMS IN BODY SENSITIVITY SCORE

Positive Statements	Negative Statements
1. Stands erect	Cowers
2. Turns head away	Does not turn head away
3. Looks at tester	Looks away from tester
4. Shows pain by action	Does not show pain
5. Comes back after pain	Struggles to get away
6. Carries tail normally	Tucks tail tightly between legs
7. Wags tail after pain	Does not wag tail after pain
8. Shows pain by cry or whimper or body movement	Growls

scores would be fairly highly correlated.

Tests in Group III: simulated guide experience. This was a group of tests given on a simulated city block, complete with curbs and various objects with which a blind person might collide and which a guide dog must learn to avoid. In the first part of the test, the Traffic test, the puppy was led down the sidewalk toward a two wheeled cart. Another person pushed the cart toward the puppy but stopped before touching him. This was repeated again at an intersection in the sidewalk. Afterwards the puppy was led up to the cart and his reaction noted. Meanwhile the scorers answered either a positively or a negatively worded series of 5 questions regarding the puppy's reaction to the moving vehicle. A good reaction was, of course, to avoid the cart without becoming fearful. Next the puppy was led across a patch of metal in the sidewalk and over a shallow curb for the Footing-Crossing test. Scoring involved two questions, chiefly as to whether the puppy recognized these two differences in footing. Finally the puppy was led towards two

Table 2.7

ITEMS IN EAR SENSITIVITY SCORE

Positive Statements	Negative Statements
1. Does not seem startled by noise	Seems startled by noise
2. Does not tremble	Trembles
3. Does not seek to escape	Seeks to escape
4. Breathing seems normal	Pants or holds breath
5. Ears stand up to check on noise	Flattens ears at sound of noise
6. Shows - by looking in direction of the sound - desire to investigate	Does not try to locate origin of sound
7. Adjusts with tail held normally or wagging	Cringes
8. Recovers confidence after investigation of sound	Does not recover confidence after sound

objects which partially or completely obstructed the sidewalk: an overhanging bar and a gate. He was also led past a pedestrian. The scorers then answered sets of three questions concerning whether the puppy noticed these three types of obstructions. This score, which has been termed Closeness, referring to the closeness to which the puppy approached these objects, actually should have been called "Reaction to Obstructions".

The Heel Test also belongs to this group, since all of the simulated traffic tests were done on the leash and were dependent on the puppy having learned to do this well. However, the actual scores for the Heel test were based on other behavior. On the first week of testing the puppy was carried to the testing room and only placed on a leash when it was returned to the kennels. Since the puppy usually wished to get back to familiar surroundings, this made an easy learning situation. On subsequent weeks the rating was made as the puppy was led to the testing area away from the kennel. Under experimental con-

ditions the reaction of a puppy to leash training is a good in-
dicator of fearfulness, as the puppy is usually being led into
strange surroundings (Scott and Fuller, 1965). In this case,
however, the test was a mild one in that the puppy was being
led into familiar surroundings which were repeated week after
week. The training differed from ordinary obedience training
in that the puppy was encouraged to move slightly ahead of the
tester, since a guide dog will always lead the blind person.
The puppy was always led on the left, again conforming to the
general practice with guide dogs.

Thus each puppy received a group of 13 scores based on 3
general test situations. The actual testing procedures were
quite simple, and the whole procedure took approximately half
an hour for each puppy. This meant that each puppy received
one half hour of training per week from 8 until 12 weeks of age.
As well as serving as a measuring device, the testing procedures
laid the foundation for the kind of simple obedience training
which the puppy would continue to receive in the 4-H home in
which he spent the next 8 or 9 months of his life.

REFERENCES

Anastasi, A. Psychological Testing, 2nd ed. New York,
    Macmillan, 1961.
Fuller, J. L. Experiential deprivation and later behavior.
    Science, 1967, 158, 1645-1652.
Fuller, J. L. & Clark, L. D. Effects of rearing with specific
    stimuli upon post-isolation behavior in dogs. Journal of
    Comparative and Physiological Psychology, 1966(a), 61,
    258-263.
Fuller, J. L. & Clark, L. D. Genetic and treatment factors
    modifying the post-isolation syndrome in dogs. Journal of
    Comparative and Physiological Psychology, 1966(b), 61,
    251-257.
Freedman, D. G., King, J. A. & Elliot, O. Critical period in
    the social development of dogs. Science, 1961, 133, 1016-
    1017.

Krushinski, L. V. Animal Behavior, Its Normal and Abnormal
    Development. New York, Consultants' Bureau, 1962.

Pfaffenberger, C. J. & Scott, J. P. The relationship between
    delayed socialization and trainability in guide dogs.
    Journal of Genetic Psychology, 1959, 95, 145-155.

Scott, J. P. Critical periods for the development of social
    behavior in dogs. In: S. Kazda and V. Denenberg (Eds.),
    The Postnatal Development of Phenotype. Prague, Academia,
    1970.

Scott, J. P. & Fuller, J. L. Genetics and the Social Behavior
    of the Dog. Chicago, University of Chicago Press, 1965.

Scott, J. P., Stewart, J. M. & DeGhett, V. J. Critical periods
    in the organization of systems. Developmental Psychobiol-
    ogy, 1974, 7, 489-513.

ANALYSIS OF THE PUPPY TESTING PROGRAM

J. P. Scott and S. W. Bielfelt

These tests and their scoring were described in Chapter 2. Since their purpose was to develop a means of selecting puppies with a special aptitude for guide dog training, they have been studied chiefly in relation to the results of training the same puppies as guides. This is the ultimate means of validating these tests, but it is at best a crude method, and is bound to give underestimates rather than overestimates of the efficiency of selection of the puppies. While the puppy testing program was set up on a scientific basis, and every effort made to be sure that every puppy received the same experience, the training program was a practical one and subject to considerable variation. As will be seen also in later chapters, the results varied from year to year, depending upon the skill of the available trainers, the turnover in training personnel, and the available number of puppies. While efforts were made to follow a standard program, any competent trainer develops his own variation of method, and it is primarily his decision as to whether it is worthwhile to continue training one dog or to go on to another which seems more promising. When there is a plentiful supply of dogs it seems more efficient to train only the most promising ones, whereas when the supply is short it is worthwhile making great efforts even with dogs of moderate abilities. It is obvious that under these circumstances there is no exact cut-off point, and that an animal with moderate capacities might be either trained or discarded, depending on the circumstances.

Furthermore, in most of the populations that we tested, both the top and bottom extremes were eliminated before guide

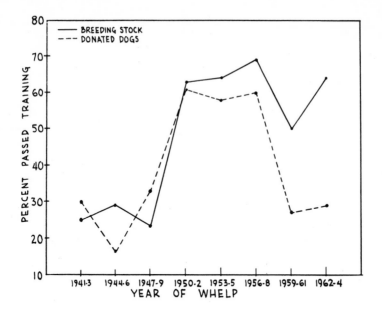

Figure 3.1. Trainers' success, by 3-year periods. During 1941-43, only 41 dogs entered training.

dog training commenced. The top scoring puppies were usually reserved for breeding, and the low scoring animals were discarded. Variance was thus reduced in the remaining population, with a corresponding reduction in the opportunity for correlation. This means that estimates of correlation are always conservative, the true figure probably being somewhat larger.

The most general fact about the training program was that before 1950 only about 30 percent of the available dogs were trained, whereas after this date more than 60 percent were trained. This level was maintained fairly consistently, except for one low period, up until the end of this research program (Fig. 3.1). The fact that the level of success with donated dogs rose and fell in the same years as did that for dogs from the breeding program indicates that circumstances other than the native quality of the puppies could vary from year to year.

First Evaluation of the Puppy Tests

When the puppy tests were originally developed the first

Table 3.1

RESULTS OF TRAINING PUPPIES FROM AN UNSELECTED SAMPLE
(Puppies tested from Nov. 28, 1949 to June 29, 1953, all breeds)

Results of Puppy Tests		Eliminated, Poor Physique		Eliminated for Behavioral Reasons			Passed Training	
				Prior to Training	In Training	Total		
Category	No.	No.	%	Training	Training	Total	No.	%
Passed	188	73	39	0	46	46	69	60
Poor	18	7	39	1	5	6	5	45
Failed	33	8	24	10	10	20	5	20
Total	239	88	37	11	61	72	79	52

task was to determine whether or not they had any predictive
value for guide dog training. With this in mind, 33 puppies
that were considered to have failed the puppy tests were saved
and run through the entire program. Table 3.1 summarizes the
results for the whole population from which this sample was
drawn. These puppies were tested between November 28, 1949,
and June 29, 1953. This was after the time when the efficiency
of training had improved, and so the puppies had a reasonably
fair chance to show their abilities. Trainers and caretakers
did not know which had passed and which had failed.

A considerable number (37% of the total) of puppies were
dropped from the program because of defects in physique. This
happened in a somewhat smaller proportion of the failed puppies.
Therefore, poor physique was probably not a cause for behavioral
failure. Later, 10 of the failed puppies and one of those rated
"poor" showed behavior that was so obviously inadequate that
they were dropped without training. The final result was, after
eliminating those puppies with defective physique, that 60% of
the puppies who had passed became guides. Those rated "poor"
had a success rate three-fourths as great, while those that had
failed showed a success rate of only one-third that of the highest group. Overall, the results are statistically significant
at the .01 level. We therefore concluded that the test had
predictive value, and it was used accordingly in selecting and

discarding puppies for future work.

In order to estimate the predictive power of the tests more precisely, correlations were calculated between puppy test success and guide dog success, using the tetrachoric r as calculated by the method of Jenkins (1955) and Fishman (1956). As with other correlation coefficients, a perfect positive correlation is 1.0, no correlation is 0.0, and a perfect negative correlation is -1.0. If the puppy tests were perfect predictors of guide dog performance, we would expect a correlation of 1.0, and, in the unlikely event that poor performance on the puppy test meant good performance as guides, the correlation should be -1.0.

The results yielded an r of .554, indicating that 31% of the variation in final success of guide dogs could be accounted for by variation in the puppy tests.

To put this in more practical terms, if all puppies that failed the test were not eliminated, four-fifths of these animals would have represented a waste of time and money, as against the two-fifths average wastage of animals that had passed the puppy tests. The odds of successfully training a dog that had passed the puppy test were approximately 3:2; those for a poor performer 1:1; while the odds for a failed puppy were only 1:4.

Since the scores from these puppies comprise the one group of available data in which the complete range of variation is present, they are also useful to determine the efficiency and predictive value of the sub-tests. Table 3.2 shows the tetrachoric r's between the scores of the sub-tests and the results of final training on all animals. The highest correlations were obtained with the Come, Fetch, and Footing-Crossing tests, all in the neighborhood of .30. While the complete calculation shown in the table was not done at the time, the relatively high correlation of the Fetch test was noticed immediately, and this part of the test was given considerable weight in the subsequent selection of breeding stock. The Intelligent Response, Willing Temperament, and Regularity tests appeared to be unsatisfactory, and were later modified. These three tests were not given after 1955. To replace them, four other tests were developed, one of which, the Willing-in-Training test, provided

Table 3.2

TETRACHORIC CORRELATIONS BETWEEN SUB-TESTS AND TRAINING SUCCESS
(Puppies tested from Nov. 28, 1949 to June 29, 1953, all breeds)

Test Group	Test	Tetrachoric r
I	Sit	-.101
	Come	.301
	Fetch	.269
	Intelligent Response*	.125
	Willing Temperament*	-.030
	Regularity*	-.033
II	Body Sensitivity	.077
	Ear Sensitivity	-.254
III	Traffic	-.007
	Footing-Crossing	.307
	Closeness	.170
	Heel	.187

*Not given to puppies whelped after 1955

---

the highest predictive value in later years. Four of the tests
(Traffic, Willing Temperament, Regularity, and Body Sensitivity)
showed correlations which were essentially zero. Two others
were negative, the Sit test and Ear Sensitivity. Heel, which
showed one of the highest predictive value in later years had
an only moderately large correlation at this time, as did Closeness. This brings up the question of whether the results of
the tests changed in succeeding years because of the selection
program aimed at improving the breeding stock.

Organization and Nature of the Tests

Relationships between test scores. The 13 tests described
in Chapter 2 comprised a test battery that was given within a
half hour period. They were consequently related to each other
in time and also in the following ways. One of the first tests
was Heeling, or training the dog to walk on a leash. This was
scored as the puppy was brought back to the kennel and was given
once a week for a total of five times. The dog also walked on

a leash while given the simulated Traffic test at 12 weeks, from which the Traffic, Footing-Crossing, and Closeness scores were derived. The final test of responses to New Experience was also given on a leash. It would be expected that the animal's ability to adapt to leash training would affect these other scores.

The tests of Traffic, Footing-Crossing, and Closeness are different scores which were given as the puppy was led through the simulated Traffic test. These scores should be correlated with each other, since they were based on episodes of behavior performed in the same situation and closely following each other in time.

In the series of tests given from 8 to 12 weeks, the puppy was first led into the testing room, where the Sit, Come, and Fetch tests were done, one after the other. We would expect that the pups would show some carry-over effect from one test to the other, and that the scores should therefore be correlated. The tests are also related more directly. For example, in the Fetch test the puppy must also "come" to the trainer with the ball. The two general scores of Trained Response and Willing-in-Training are based on behavior in this situation and therefore belong in this group.

The two tests of Body Sensitivity and Ear Sensitivity were then given in an outside testing area. Two additional scores of New Experience Response and Willing-New-Experience were based on the same behavior. These four scores were therefore closely related, both in time and place.

The 13 scores in the test thus fall into 3 groups, based on 3 test situations (See Table 3.3).

Correlational relationships. Correlation coefficients (Pearson product-moment) were calculated between the puppy test scores of approximately 300 puppies born in 1958-59. When 209 of these were later trained, 120 passed and 89 failed. The original group of 300 puppies should therefore have included a good range of capacities.

The results are shown in Table 3.3. There was a total number of 78 possible correlations, of which 44 were large enough to be considered statistically significant at less than .05.

Table 3.3

CORRELATIONS BETWEEN PUPPY TEST SCORES

(300 puppies whelped 1958–59; 209 trained)

Test Group	Sit	Come	Fetch	T.R.	W.T.	B.S.	E.S.	NER	WNE	T.	F.C.	C.	Heel
I Sit		.292**	.143*	-.023	-.028	-.195**	-.072	-.017	-.004	-.006	-.044	-.109	-.018
Come			.278**	.130*	.181**	.107	.101	.165**	.197**	.100	.117*	.151**	.200**
Fetch				.313**	.292**	.078	.062	.152**	.148**	.061	.073	.015	.112
Trained Response					.830	.291**	.073	.318**	.336**	.013	.028	.018	.123*
Willing-in-Training						.275**	.250**	.346**	.354**	.006	.094	.115**	.199**
II Body Sensitivity							.208*	.375**	.588**	.077	.054	.070	.271**
Ear Sensitivity								.310**	.337**	.033	.118*	.092	.070
New Experience Response									.537**	-.037	-.016	.097	.199**
Willing-New-Experience										.115*	.124	.077	.270**
III Traffic											.462**	.296**	.258**
Footing-Crossing												.445**	.311**
Closeness													.292**
Heel													

*P<.05   **P<.01

Only 3.9 correlations of this magnitude would be expected by chance alone. The scores are therefore correlated with each other to a large extent.

Table 3.3 shows the number of significant correlations for each test score. With the exception of the Sit test, all tests show close to the maximum number of correlations with tests in the same group, as might be expected. In addition, four of the tests show a large number of correlations with other tests, whether closely related or not. Two of them, Come and Heel, were tests of trained performance, while the two others, Willing-in-Training and Willing-New-Experience, were scores based on emotional responses. The last two were also related to each other because of being based on the same test form applied in two situations.

At the opposite extreme was the Sit test, significantly correlated with only three other tests, two of which belong in the same test group. If correlations with tests in the same group are disregarded, the Fetch, Ear Sensitivity, and Closeness scores also showed a considerable degree of independence.

Within the three groups of tests, each containing tests related to each other through time and place and whose correlations are found in triangular groups in Table 3.3, significant correlations were found between every pair of scores but two, those between Sit and Trained Response, and Sit and Willing-in-Training. These within-group correlations account for 20 of the 44 significant correlations and form additional evidence for dividing the tests into three groups.

Considering the scores group by group, in Group I the Sit, Come, and Fetch scores were moderately highly correlated, with the lowest correlation between Sit and Fetch. Sit, itself, showed only one other significant correlation, a negative one with Body Sensitivity. This presumably meant that an overly sensitive (and thus low scoring) pup responded quickly to being forced into the Sit position. The Sit score is thus the most independent of any in the whole group. The Trained Response and Willing-in-Training scores were highly correlated with each other, and both were most highly correlated with Fetch, a task in which the puppy had the most freedom of action, and least with Sit, which consisted of completely forced training.

The three scores given on the simulated Traffic test (Group III) were moderately highly correlated with each other but still relatively independent. They also ranked close to Sit in being the least correlated with other tests. This may result in part from the fact that this test was given only once and in a different location from the rest. The other test in this group, Heel, was, as might be expected, correlated with a large number of tests outside the group.

Finally, the scores on sensitivity and response to new experience (Group II) showed correlations with each other that ranged from low to moderately high. The two highest correlations both involved Willing-New-Experience, one with Body Sensitivity, and the other with New Experience Response.

The significant correlations between groups, seen in the data of Table 3.3 as rectangular groups, are smaller and less numerous, with the greatest number between Groups I and II, which were given each week. The highest correlations were found between the four scores of Trained Response, New Experience Response, Willing-New-Experience, and Willing-in-Training. The two "response" scores were entered on similar score sheets, as were the two "willing" scores, and this probably accounted for some of the correlation.

Factor analysis. The above conclusions were confirmed by a factor analysis (Yates, 1967, private communication). This well-known statistical technique makes it possible to analyze correlation tables in terms of groups of related tests as well as in pairs. The results of this analysis, using the principle-axis technique and machine computation, are shown in Table 3.4. Factor 1 included all four of the tests of Group III, and Factor 2 similarly included the four tests in Group I. However, the analysis breaks down the Group I tests into two factors. The first of these might well be called the "Sit-Come" factor, since these two tests received high loadings. The Fetch test received a low loading on this factor and also in Factor 4. We have already pointed out that the Fetch test was related to training to Come in that part of the training in playful retrieving required the dog to come to the experimenter.

Factor 4 emphasizes the ratings on Trained Response and

Table 3.4

PRINCIPAL AXIS FACTORS DERIVED FROM PUPPY TESTS

Test	Factor Loading
Factor 1--Group II Tests	
Willing-New-Experience	.82
Body Sensitivity	.73
New Experience Response	.72
Ear Sensitivity	.59
Factor 2--Group III Tests	
Footing-Crossing	.81
Closeness	.72
Traffic	.71
Heel	.55
Factor 3--"Sit-Come" Factor	
Sit	.80
Come	.73
Fetch	.47
Factor 4--Motivation	
Trained Response	.92
Willing-in-Training	.88
Fetch	.49

Willing-in-Training and might therefore be called a "motivation" factor. The fact that Fetch also appears in this factor indicates that the other two ratings are largely based on performance in the Fetch test.

As will be seen in the next section, the efficiency of these various tests for distinguishing between dogs that pass or fail in future training as guide dogs changed as the tests were repeated. However, the efficiency of the Trained Response and Willing-in-Training tests remained quite high from week to week, and since most of the final test scores were based on the final week's performance, these scores had a higher predictive value than those whose efficiency gradually declined. For example, the predictive power of the Fetch test tended to decrease with repeated training, probably because all dogs reached much the same level of performance in the end. Since

this was the test which was most closely related to the Trained
Response and Willing-in-Training scores, this probably means
that the raters obtained an early impression of the way the puppies reacted and retained it even after the performance had
changed.

It is also interesting to look at those tests which received low factor loadings. These tests were the least highly
correlated with the others, and therefore had the greatest possibility of measuring some unique behavior characteristic.
There were three of these tests, one from each group: Ear Sensitivity, Heel, and Fetch. In each of these, approximately
65% of the variance was not accounted for by correlation with
other tests.

Weekly changes in predictability of future performance.
The final puppy test scores as used in the selection program
were, in the case of the training tests (Sit, Fetch, Come, and
Heel), based on the final level of proficiency attained by the
puppies, whereas other scores were based on the average through
several weeks (See Chapter 2). In previous work (Scott and
Fuller, 1965), we found that, as a result of repetitive training, puppies might either become more alike, more unlike, or
might remain the same, relative to each other. The weekly
scores were therefore examined with these possibilities in mind.

This analysis was based on 494 dogs that were whelped during the 3 years 1958 to 60, and that were subsequently given
the puppy tests. Of these, 330 were eventually trained and
were divided into two groups: those that became guides (174)
and those that failed because of behavioral reasons (156). As
shown in Figure 3.2, the average score during each week of
training was computed for each of the subtests. Similar average scores were computed for the puppies that had passed or
failed, and the "t" value computed for each difference. (The
larger the value of this statistic the less the probability
that the differences were obtained by chance). Changes in these
values are shown on tne graphs. To interpret them it must be
remembered that a "t" value of 2.0 is equivalent to a statistical probability figure of .05. Therefore only those values of
2.0 or greater indicate that the test had a high predictive

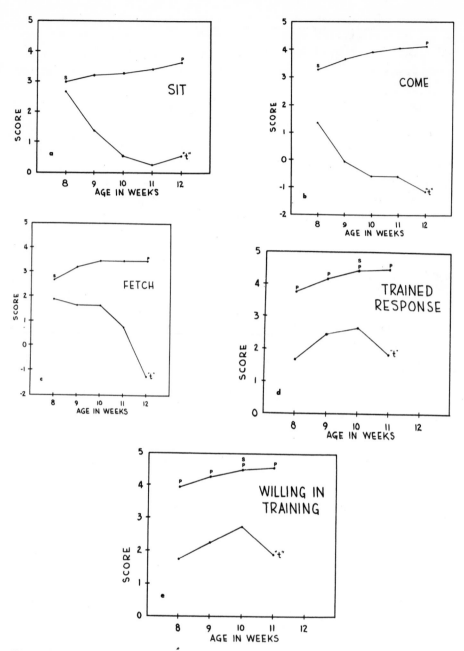

Figure 3.2, a-e. Weekly averages and "t" scores for Group I tests. ("P" = scores previously used; "S" = scores having highest predictability). Note that while the performance gets better as the puppies grow older and have more training, the predictive value of the score may decrease.

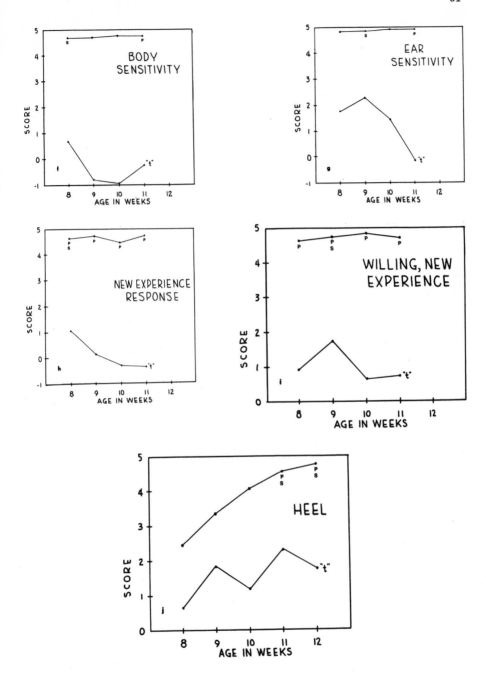

Figure 3.2, f-j. Weekly averages and "t" scores for Group II and Heel tests. Except for Ear Sensitivity and Heel, the predictive value of these tests is low.

value.

The results are quite obvious from a glance at the figures. All of the tests in Group II, which are chiefly tests of emotional responses to new situations, gave quite high average scores that showed no change from week to week. One test in Group I, the Sit test, also showed little improvement, but the average scores were consistently intermediate. In all of these tests, the best "t" values were found at either the first or second week of testing. That is, the initial response of the puppy to these tests gave the best indication of future performance.

All the other tests in Group I--Come, Trained Response, Willing-in-Training, and Fetch--showed a gradual improvement in performance over the initial trial. The Fetch test was somewhat different in that all the improvement came in the first 3 trials. Both the Come and Fetch scores, however, show the best predictability on the initial trial, declining precipitously as the animal grew older. The point is, of course, that continued training probably brought all dogs up to the same level of performance, after which the test had little predictive value. The Trained Response and Willing-in-Training ratings, which were based on this performance, show rising "t" values up until week 10, after which they decline.

The Heel test is markedly different from the others in that it shows an unusually strong improvement from week to week, with the "t" score fluctuating, but with a general tendency to rise rather than fall. With this one exception, all of the puppy test scores that are repeated provide the best predictive value at the first trial or shortly thereafter.

In Table 3.5 we provide a scheme for using the puppy test subscores in ways that give maximum predictability. It will be noted (Figure 3.2) that the newly recommended scores agree with those previously used only in the case of the Heel tests. The "t" values for some of the previously used scores actually fell below zero, notably in the Come, Fetch, Body Sensitivity, and New-Experience-Response scores, indicating that the scores at that point were beginning to be negatively correlated with guide dog success.

The scores of the tests in Group III, which were given only

Table 3.5

SUGGESTED SCORING SYSTEM FOR BEST PREDICTIVE VALUE

Sub-test	Highest "t" value	Score to be Used, Weeks	Suggested Weight
High Weight			
Willing-in-Training	2.8	10	1.0
Trained Response	2.6	10	1.0
Sit	2.5	8	1.0
Heel	2.2	11-12	1.0
Ear Sensitivity	2.2	9	1.0
Intermediate Weight			
Fetch	1.8	8	.9
Willing-New-Experience	1.8	9	.9
Come	1.3	8	.8
Low Weight			
New Experience Response	1.0	8	.7
Body Sensitivity	.8	8	.5
Traffic	-.04	12	.0
Footing-Crossing	-.06	12	.0
Closeness	.03	12	.0

on the last week of testing, had almost no predictive value for the dogs in the sample given. In other words, all of the puppies behaved about the same on this test, and its utility for this purpose is questionable. However, this test should not be discarded without confirming these results on another group of dogs, particularly since the Footing-Crossing test gave one of the highest correlations with success in the original unselected sample of puppies. Those on which this analysis was based had had both the worst and best performers eliminated before final training, and it is possible that the Footing-Crossing test could be valuable in detecting puppies that were markedly deviant in either direction.

A further device for using the scores to the best advantage is given in Table 3.5. Weights for the different scores are assigned in accordance with probability tables, so that any combined score for a puppy will give a more accurate prediction. When these tests are begun at different ages (the puppy testing program at San Rafael currently begins at 6 weeks), their predictability should be recalculated, as the age at the first experience may be as important as the first experience itself.

Heritability of the Puppy Test Scores

The success of any selection program is obviously dependent on whether or not the traits selected are inherited. In actuality, no traits can be biologically inherited as such. Rather, the population in a new generation receives a sample of the genes and cytoplasm of the preceding generation. The effects of these genes can be calculated only by determining the change in variation of a trait as it is affected by changes in genetic variation in the population tested. Variation is usually measured in terms of the variance (or squared standard deviation) of the population. Theoretically, anywhere from 0 to 100% of the variance could be the result of genetic variation, but in practice this is usually 50% or less. Even if only a small percentage of the variance is affected by heredity, a selection program will have some effect.

In estimating the effect of heredity, the problem is to identify the environmental and hereditary components which make up the variance. In most practical cases this can never be done with complete accuracy, but we can distinguish portions of the variance that should be largely environmental, and other portions that should be largely hereditary.

Results of analysis of variance. This analysis was done on the group of puppies born from 1958 to 1964. In the first analysis only those 236 puppies were used that came from repeated matings where two or more full sib litters had been born and the resulting puppies tested. These matings included 9 German shepherd, 5 golden retriever, and 2 Labrador retriever pairings. Thus it was possible to determine the amount of variance within litters, which is partly due to hereditary differences between individuals but also in part to small differences in the environment, and to separate this from the amount of variance caused by differences between litters in the same mating, which should be largely due to environmental differences in rearing and test-

Table 3.6

VARIANCE COMPONENTS OF PUPPY TEST SCORES
(Puppies Whelped 1958-64 in Repeat Matings; n=236)

			Percentage of Variance			
Group	Test Score	Total Variance	Within Litters	Between Litters	Between Matings	Between Breeds
I	Sit	.82	69	22**	.7	3
	Come	.51	77	13*	10	0
	Fetch	.71	78	8	10	5
	Trained Response	.46	71	8	27**	-6
	Willing-in-Training	.42	63	12*	33**	-7
	Average		72	13	17	-1
II	Body Sensitivity	.27	79	21**	3	-3
	Ear Sensitivity	.13	75	11	19*	-4
	New Ex. Response	.36	83	10	9	-2
	Willing-New-Ex.	.26	72	28**	1	-1
	Average		77	18	8	-3
III	Traffic	.48	87	3	4	6
	Footing-Crossing	.50	73	10	0	16
	Closeness	.59	86	22**	-12	3
	Heel	.62	74	17*	1	9
	Average		80	13	-2	9
All Tests	Average		76	14	9	1

*P < .05
**P < .01

ing. The remaining variance can be divided between that which is associated with differences between matings and that between breeds. Since most of the environmental variance has been extracted, these last two components should be largely hereditary.

Variance components were estimated according to the method of Gower (1962). In this method the individual and environmental components are extracted first. If these are overestimated, negative figures will sometimes be obtained for the remaining variance. The method thus tends to underestimate the effects of heredity. This is in addition to the fact that an unknown portion of the within-litter variance may also be due to heredity. The method thus gives a conservative estimate of the effects of heredity.

As seen in Table 3.6, the amounts of total variance were largest in the scores of Group I, being especially large in the Sit and Fetch tests. Those scores in Group III were next largest, and those in Group II were the smallest of all, especially that of Ear Sensitivity, where the variance was only about 13% of what it might have been with a theoretically ideal distribution. None of the scores showed a variance as high as 1.0, which would be expected with an ideal distribution (See Chapter 2).

Averaging all scores together, 76% of the variance could be ascribed to individual differences, 14% to environmental differences between litters, 9% to differences between matings, and 1% to differences between breeds. The differences between breeds were negligible, and none of them approached statistical significance. This contrasts with the results obtained by Scott and Fuller (1965) in their experiments, where breed differences were highly important and averaged approximately 27%. Their results, however, were based on a group of breeds that had been chosen for maximum differences in behavior, whereas the three breeds used as guide dogs had been chosen for their ability to perform this particular task, and hence for their similarity. Also, the Jackson Laboratory populations were based on a small sample of one or two original matings from each breed, as opposed to the somewhat larger samples in the guide dog study. In either case, there are large overlaps between breeds with respect to behavior. The largest breed differences appeared in the scores of Group III, including the simulated Traffic and Heel tests.

Differences between matings showed a different picture. The largest differences were found in Group I tests, these being about twice as great as those in Group II, whereas those in Group III were essentially zero. This means that the genetic variance within breeds was largely concentrated in the test scores of Group I. That of Ear Sensitivity in Group II showed a large percentage, but this was based on a very small total variance and therefore has little practical value, even if it is a real effect. Within Group I, the Trained Response and Willing-in-Training scores showed the largest effects. These were the tests which had the highest predictability for guide dog success and were also those which involved emotional reactions during training. The Come and Fetch tests showed the next largest amounts of between-mating variance, although these were not statistically significant.

Seven of the thirteen test scores showed significantly large amounts of variance that could be attributed to differences between litters. There was little difference between the test groups in this respect, and the average percentage of 14% corresponded quite closely to that obtained by Scott and Fuller (1965). In their study of segregating populations from a basenji-cocker spaniel cross, they found that 76% of the variance could be attributed to differences within litters, 12% between litters, and 12% between matings. In the present study the corresponding figures were 76%, 14%, 9%, plus 1% attributable to breed differences.

As a check on these calculations, which involved only a small portion of the total number of puppies tested, a second set of computations was made on a population of 869 puppies born in the same years 1958-64, including all puppies tested whose sires had produced puppies from more than one dam (Table 3.7). Puppies from 34 sires and 105 dams were included in this analysis. Variance components were calculated for differences between individuals coming from the same mother, differences between puppies born to different dams, differences between puppies born to different sires, and finally differences between breeds. This calculation did not separate environmental and hereditary components as well as the previous one, since the between-litter variance was left in all components.

The between-sire component should be the most clearly related to heredity, since the sires had no contact with their offspring. The calculation does permit a comparison between maternal and paternal effects. The between-dam component was over three times as large as the heritability figure based on sires, indicating an important effect of the maternal environment.

As with the previous table, the between-breed components were very small, and none of them are significant. The average between-sire component was about 5%. Since the sire contributes only half the variable heredity to the offspring, this

Table 3.7

VARIANCE COMPONENTS OF PUPPY TEST SCORES

(Puppies Whelped 1958-64; n=869;
from sires mated to more than one dam)

Group	Test Score	Total Variance	Percentage of Variance			
			Within Dams	Between Dams	Between Sires	Between Breeds
I	Sit	.95	66	27**	3	4
	Come	.52	80	14**	7*	0
	Fetch	.97	76	9**	12**	4
	Trained Response	.56	67	27**	4	3
	Willing-in-Training	.42	66	27**	6	0
	Average		71	21	6	2
II	Body Sensitivity	.25	72	20**	8*	0
	Ear Sensitivity	.14	80	20**	0	0
	New Ex. Response	.43	75	23**	3	-1
	Willing-New-Ex.	.33	74	16**	12**	-2
	Average		75	20	6	-1
III	Traffic	.43	82	11**	6	2
	Footing-Crossing	.44	79	18**	3	0
	Closeness	.51	87	12**	2	-1
	Heel	.76	80	9**	5*	6
	Average		82	13	4	2
All Tests	Average		76	18	5	1

*P < .05
**P < .01

figure should be half as great as that contributed by both parents and seen in Table 3.6 as between-mating variance. This latter figure averaged 9%, almost twice that for the sires, so that the general figures are in good agreement.

On the other hand, the results with particular tests do not agree as well (Table 3.8). The two scores of Trained Response and Willing-in-Training, which showed the highest between mating scores, showed only small effects between sires and large ones between dams. These scores are therefore strongly affected by the maternal environment, either pre- or post-natally. Thus, emotional reactions of the puppy were affected much more by the dam than by the sire.

The Fetch score showed one of the largest sire effects,

Table 3.8

PERCENTAGE OF VARIANCE ATTRIBUTABLE TO
DIFFERENCES IN PARENTAL HEREDITY

Group	Test Score	Between Sires x 2	Between Matings
I	Sit	6	7
	Come	14	10
	Fetch	24	10
	Trained Response	8	27
	Willing-in-Training	12	33
	Average	13	17
II	Body Sensitivity	16	3
	Ear Sensitivity	0	19
	New Ex. Response	6	9
	Willing-New-Ex.	24	1
	Average	12	8
III	Traffic	12	4
	Footing-Crossing	6	0
	Closeness	4	-12
	Heel	10	1
	Average	8	-2
All Tests	Average	11	9

approximately 12%, and this agrees with the original observations that certain sires had a large effect on this score in their offspring. This score also showed one of the lowest effects between dams, and in Table 3.6 showed a low percentage of between-litter variance that can be attributed to the environment. The data are thus consistent with the conclusion that this score was probably the most highly heritable in the whole series.

One other score had a high between-sire value, that for Willing-New-Experience. This, however, disagreed with the between-mating variance, which is very low. The apparent differences between offspring of different dams and sires can be accounted for by the non-genetic between-litter variance, which is quite large in this test.

The between-dam variance figures for all scores were quite high, averaging about 18%. If we subtract 14%, the figure calculated on Table 3.6 for environmental between-litter variance, this figure closely approached that of the sires. Making such a correction for the individual tests, however, leads to inconsistent results.

The figures for total variance in this large population approached the 1.0 level (corresponding to the ideal distribution described in Chapter 2) in both the Sit and Fetch tests, and the Fetch test had the highest figure of all (Table 3.7). The only other score that had a relatively high figure was that for Heel. In the rest of the test scores, the variance that is available for genetic selection is restricted by about 50% or more. Undoubtedly, much of this results from the nature of the scoring system, which has an absolute upper limit. When many of the puppies were scored as 4's and 5's, as happened in many tests, the variance was correspondingly reduced.

In general, this analysis indicates that on the average there was about 10% of genetic variance available for selection. As pointed out above, this is probably an understatement. The data also indicate that the greatest amount of genetic variance was found in the test scores of Group I, especially the Come and Fetch tests. Finally, there is the interesting possibility that the test scores involving emotionality were greatly affected by the maternal environment. Since undesirable emotional reactions create one of the greatest practical problems involved in training, this possibility should be followed up in future research. Since the dam normally has no contact with her pups after weaning, these effects must either be produced in the early weeks of life, or possibly in prenatal life, or both.

Changes in Test Scores During the Selection Program

After the tests were developed and validated, they were given in their original form from the middle of 1953 to the middle of 1955. In 1955 the final form of the test was introduced and was given to all animals tested in 1956. From that time on there was no change in the form of the tests and very few changes in the personnel of the testers. In January 1958, the procedure of socializing the puppies at 6 and 7 weeks, prior to the regular testing program, was introduced. This would be expected to improve those scores of the puppy tests which depend on a friendly relationship with the handler, especially the Come and Fetch tests.

In addition, the puppies from 1953 onward were being increasingly bred from a stock which had been selected for good performance on the Fetch and Traffic tests. This should have resulted in improvement in these scores and also that of the Come test, which was closely related to Fetch training.

This was actually the case, but since there was a good deal of year-to-year variability which probably resulted from small numbers, the scores have been combined over three-year periods as shown in Figures 3.3-3.5.

The overall score (Fig. 3.4) showed a general improvement over the first three periods with a slight decline in the fourth, and most of the individual tests follow the same pattern. The Fetch score provides some of the most crucial evidence for effects of selection, since it shows high heritability and little evidence of any maternal effect. It shows a marked improvement over the first three periods, rising in a straight line. The total improvement consists of 1.6 points on the 6-point scale in 9 years, or 32 percent of the total scale.

Changes closely similar to the Fetch score are seen in the Come and Heel tests. Data is not available for the two first three-year periods for the Trained Response and Willing-in-Training tests and their corresponding forms in Group II, but the latter portions of their curves appear to be similar.

Changes in the other tests take a different form--an initial steep rise that gradually becomes smaller as if approaching an asymptote at 1959-61, with no falling off in the final period.

In Group II the curves for Body Sensitivity and Ear Sensitivity take this form. In Group III, the curve for Traffic is quite similar, except that it falls off in the final period. Footing-Crossing and Closeness also follow the same general form.

The one test that was outstandingly different from the others was the Sit test, whose average scores remained on essentially the same level throughout the entire 15 years. This test was one of forced training, and almost all puppies learned to sit at a fairly high level of proficiency. It was also the

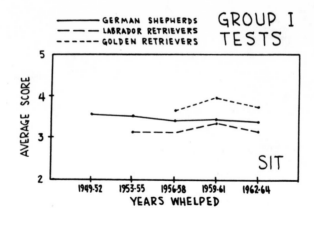

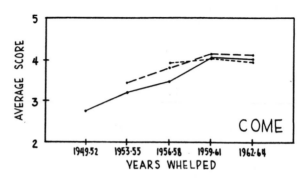

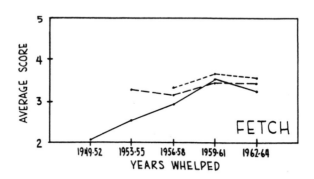

Figure 3.3. Changes in Group I test scores in response to selection in the three major breeds. Note that the Fetch score,
which had a relatively high heritability and was given much
weight in the selection process, rose steadily through 1959-61.
Other correlated scores show similar curves. The Sit score,
which was only weakly correlated with Fetch, showed essentially
no change.

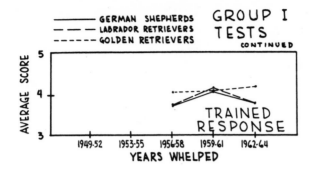

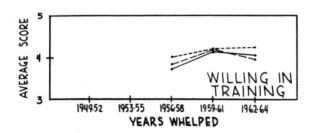

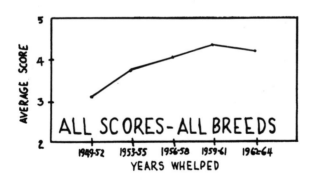

Figure 3.3 (continued). The composite score for all tests in Groups I, II, and III reflects the fact that most of the test scores improved under the selection program.

least highly correlated with all other tests. These two facts probably explain the fact that no changes in it occurred.

There are three possible hypotheses that could account for these results. One is that the selection program did indeed produce improvements. Another is that there was an improvement in training methods accompanied by some relaxation in grading standards (similar to the so-called "grade inflation" reported on college campuses in recent years), or there may have been a combination of both. There was some suspicion among the workers that the latter had taken place and an effort was made to rank the puppies more stringently, which may account for the fall in some test scores during the last period.

If such a relaxation of standards did take place, it did not affect all tests equally. The Sit test remained unchanged, and those tests most closely related to performance (Fetch, Come, and Heel) changed in a different fashion from the rest. The Fetch and Come tests are those that consistently have a relatively high index of heritability throughout the analysis. We can therefore conclude that while there may have been some changes in ranking standards, there was also an appreciable result of selection.

The results are thus consistent with the hypothesis that selection should bring about changes in performance on the puppy tests. These changes are of necessity slow, as a breeding bitch may produce puppies over a period of 5 or 6 years, and a male may be fathering puppies for 6 or 8 years or longer. Thus, the entire period of the experiment may cover only 3 generations in many cases. We would expect also that selection would produce the greatest changes within two generations and more slowly thereafter. The slight decline in the final three-year period may represent the fact that the genetic variation in the population had been largely exhausted, or it may also mean that most of the high producing stock selected in the first years of the program had quit producing puppies.

Given that the genetic potential of these stocks did improve, the upward changes in the puppy test scores were not accompanied by a similar upward trend in the percentage of dogs passing training, which fluctuated around the same level over the same 15-year period, with a particularly low point in years

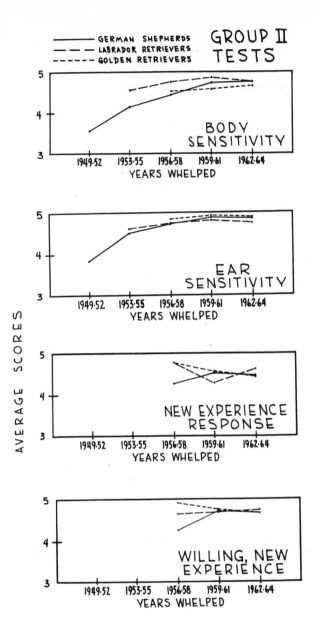

Figure 3.4. Changes in Group II scores during the selection program. Scores for these emotional responses tended to rise and approach an asymptote during later years.

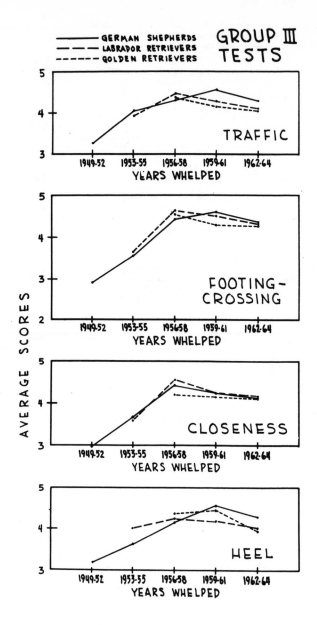

Figure 3.5. Changes in Group III scores. The most important of these is the Heel score, which has relatively high heritability and predictability values. Its curve is very similar to that of Fetch in Figure 3.3.

1959-61 (Fig. 3.1). This raises the question of the relationship between the puppy tests and final training.

Relationship of Puppy Tests to Results
with Final Training

As indicated above, there has been an opportunity to make
only one good test of the validity of the puppy tests as predictors of success in training. In this population 14% of the animals failed the puppy tests. Since three fifths of the puppies
that passed the test became guide dogs, and only one-fifth of
those that failed, the latter had only one-third as good a
chance of becoming guide dogs as the former.

As soon as this conclusion was reached in 1953, a dual
program of selection was begun. On the one hand, about 10% of
the puppies tested were failed and discarded each year without
further training. At the other extreme of the population, a
somewhat smaller percentage of the best performing animals were
saved out as breeding stock. The result was that only a cur-
tailed population of more or less average dogs was available
for further studies of the effectiveness of the puppy testing
program. It would be expected that the correlation between the
puppy tests and guide dog success would be reduced, and this is
borne out by the figures. In the years 1953-55, 11 out of 13
tests showed significant correlations with success in training.
In subsequent 3-year periods, this figure never rose above 4.
This is still better than what might be expected by pure chance,
but it is obvious that the consistent removal of the best and
worst extremes had the expected effect in the remaining populations of reducing the correlation between puppy tests and performance.

Causes of failure of guide dogs. As part of the training
procedure each trainer graded his animals on their performance,
and many of these grades had the same names as those of the puppy test scores. As shown in Table 3.9, the correlations between
corresponding test scores were extremely low and even negative
in some cases. However, there was some degree of correspondence
between trainer test scores and puppy test scores. Out of a

Table 3.9

CORRELATIONS BETWEEN PUPPY TESTS AND TRAINERS'
SCORES HAVING SIMILAR NAMES

Group I

Sit	-.03
Come	.03
Fetch	-.07
Trained Response	.18**
Willing-in-Training	.03

Group II

Body Sensitivity	.04
Ear Sensitivity	-.03
New Experience Response	Not Scored on Adults
Willing-New-Experience	Not Scored on Adults

Group III

Traffic	-.25**
Footing-Crossing	-.05
Closeness	-.07
Heel	Not Scored on Adults

**Significant at $<.01$

total of 143 correlations, 29 were significant at $<.05$, four times as many as would be expected by pure chance (7.15). Trainers and puppy testers were therefore looking at the same traits but recorded them in different scores. Fortunately, there is a more direct way of tracing the causes of failure.

The trainer also recorded the reasons why he rejected an animal. A study of the records shows that these reasons had almost no relationship to the grades given to the dog on performance. An animal might be performing perfectly satisfactorily according to the scoring system and then be discarded. For this reason a study was made of the reasons given for rejecting animals. The results for the German shepherd breed are summarized in Table 3.10. Sometimes only one reason was given and sometimes four or five. The major reason for rejecting a dog was fearfulness, which occurred in nearly half the dogs rejected. The next highest category was that of being easily distracted during work, usually by cats, dogs, and other animals and objects. This correlates with the 4-H reports (Chapter 5), in which dogs that were reported to be distracted before they

Table 3.10

REASONS GIVEN BY TRAINERS FOR
REJECTING DOGS IN TRAINING

(121 German Shepherds Whelped 1958-61)

Category	Description	Number of Cases Reported	Percent Occurrence In 121 Dogs	Percent Rejected for Sole Reason
Fearful	Shy, nervous, over-cautious, wary, apprehensive, high-strung, unsure, trembles	55	45	17
Distract-ible	Inattentive, easily distracted by cats, dogs, etc.	36	30	7
Irregular	Unpredictable, erratic, flighty	32	26	3
Irrespon-sible	Will not take responsibility for blind person	27	22	2
Over-aggressive	"Sharp"-snaps, over-protective, possessive, growls, barks	18	15	4
Correction	Reaction either too strong--hypersensitive; or too weak--unresponsive	17	14	0
Motivation	Lacks initiative, unwilling to work	14	12	1
Pulling	Pulls too fast or too hard; or too slow and too soft; or pulls irregularly	8	7	2
Urination	Urinates while working or while in house	6	5	2
Noisy	Barks; vocalizes while working	6	5	1
Bad Habits	Fence jumper; vomits food; filth eater; poor eater	4	3	1
	TOTAL REASONS GIVEN	223		

came in for training had a poor chance of success. Another important category was that of being unpredictable in work, the animal doing well one day and poorly another and being described as "irregular".

Approximately 20% of the dogs were failed because they did not take responsibility for the blind person but worked well only under direction.

Fifteen percent of the failures were reported to be over-aggressive, attempting to guard the blind person and growling and barking at other people. Approximately the same percentage of animals responded unsatisfactorily to correction. Twelve percent of the animals were reported to be lacking in motivation, and simply did not work hard enough. The remainder of the reasons referred to particular motor habits which were undesirable, although at least one of them, urination, was likely to be an emotional response.

We can conclude that the major reasons for rejecting guide dogs were not defects in intelligence but undesirable emotional reactions, and that most of these were connected with agonistic behavior, the animals being either too fearful or too aggressive and being unable to conform to the ideal of an alert but calm individual. Compared to ordinary dogs, the mature, trained guide dog impresses one as being calm, quiet, and orderly, alert but minding his own business, and being willing and responsive to people.

There was among the puppy tests no score that corresponded exactly to these reasons for rejection. However, that score designated as Willing-in-Training was largely concerned with emotional reactions. The puppy which received a low score was nervous, unfriendly, vocalized frequently, and was likely to urinate and "freeze". As indicated earlier, this test score had the highest predictive value of any, particularly in the second and third week of testing. The predictability of the puppy tests could be improved by adding a test or tests that would more directly measure undesirable emotional reactions, particularly fearfulness, distractibility, over-aggressiveness, and the like.

Summary

Success in the training program is the ultimate test of
the capacity to become a guide dog. However, there was no exact cut-off point in this program. Very poor dogs were always
eliminated, and very good ones were always successfully trained;
but among the intermediate group, variations in the supply of
puppies might determine whether or not it was efficient to train
a particular dog with borderline ability; and, of course, the
skill of trainers might vary somewhat because of changes in personnel. The outstanding change in training success came in a
relatively short period. Efficiency jumped from 30% in the
1947-49 period to 60% in the 1950-52 period. This improvement
was accompanied by the selection of better breeding stock, the
organization of the puppy testing program, the improvement of
organization of the 4-H program, prompt shifting of puppies into this program at 12 weeks and by the improvement of the final
training program and the upgrading of its personnel. It is,
therefore, difficult to ascertain the part which each of these
changes played in producing the improvement in training success.
In all probability, all of these factors had important effects.
This meant that the effects of the puppy testing program, aside
from an early validation study covering puppies tested during
the period when the trainers' success rose markedly, had to be
analyzed largely from internal evidence.

During this first evaluation of the puppy tests, 33 out of
239 puppies tested were failed, and 18 were considered poor or
borderline. Of the 33, 8 were later eliminated because of physical reasons, leaving a total of 25. Of these, 10 were eliminated from the program because of obvious behavioral defects
prior to training, and 10 more failed in training. Thus, four-
fifths of the failed puppies were unsuccessful as compared with
two-fifths of those that had passed the test. Of those that
were considered poor or borderline, more than half (6 out of 11)
were unsuccessful. The failed puppies were regularly eliminated
from the program in following years, and the same percentage of
success in final training was maintained for all dogs entering
training. However, it should be remembered that approximately
10% of the highest scoring puppies were regularly retained for

breeding stock. If this had not been the case, there might
have been a higher percentage of success in subsequent years.

In the same original population of puppies, an analysis
was made of the correlation between sub-tests and final success.
Of the 12 sub-tests given at that time, three (Come, Fetch, and
Footing-Crossing) showed relatively high positive correlations.
Two sub-tests (Heel and Closeness) showed moderately high correlations. Three of the sub-tests were considered unsatisfactory and abandoned, one having a low correlation and two being
essentially zero. The remaining tests either showed correlations that were essentially zero or negative. On this basis,
the Fetch score was given extra weight in the selection of
breeding stock.

The sub-tests themselves fell into three groups. Group I
included performance tests--Sit, Come and Fetch--and related
scores. Group II included emotional reactions to novel stimuli--
Body Sensitivity, Ear Sensitivity, and related scores. Group
III consisted of the scores based on simulated guide dog experience, plus Heel. A factor analysis based on correlations between the sub-tests confirmed these groupings.

Subsequent studies of the puppy tests were, by necessity,
based on animals with intermediate scores, including neither
the puppies that failed nor those that did extremely well. In
these studies, only the Heel test held up well as a predictor
of success among the puppies with intermediate ability. However, it developed that in most of the tests, the best predictive score was that shown by the puppies during their first
trials. If such a modified scoring system had been used, the
Come, Fetch, and Heel tests would have continued to be good
predictors. Surprisingly, Sit and Ear Sensitivity would also
have been good predictors. The simulated Traffic tests had no
predictive value in this later sample of intermediate puppies.

While this has been the first serious attempt with dogs to
predict future behavior from early tests, the problem is a common one in human affairs, and this enables us to see the results
in perspective. Perhaps the most directly comparable human
situation is that of attempting to predict student success in a
university graduate school on the basis of previous performance
(Willingham, 1974). The undergraduate grade point average,

which uses a 5 point grading scale of A, B, C, D, F, very much
like that of the puppy tests (and indeed the puppy testing grading was derived from it) correlates with future success at about
.18. Of course, this figure would undoubtedly be a good deal
higher if all undergraduates went on to graduate school. The
students who are allowed to go on to advanced work usually come
from the higher ranking undergraduates, just as only the higher
ranking puppies are allowed to go on to guide dog training.
Even so, the correlation between previous performance and future
success is very low.

When students are tested with tests designed by using the
most sophisticated techniques for test development, the results
are somewhat better. Scores on the Graduate Record Examinations
correlate at about .35 with future success. The best predictor
that Willingham was able to devise, a composite of the grade
point average and the Graduate Record Examination, achieved a
correlation of only .40. This is in spite of the fact that college students are adults and have been trained in the school
system for many years, hence their behavior should be highly
consistent and predictable. Compared with such results, the
best figure that was obtained in the puppy testing program, a
correlation of .55 between puppy test success and guide dog
success, on the sample in which the low scoring puppies were
included, looks pretty good.

In conclusion, research on the puppy testing program was
related to two problems. One was the usefulness of the tests
for predicting future success as guide dogs. The results showed
that the puppy tests were reasonably good predictors of future
success, especially when compared to similar efforts to predict
human behavior. The research also indicated that the predictive value of the puppy tests could be greatly improved, first
by using scores of the sub-tests at ages when they give the maximum predictive value rather than at the times that were originally selected, and second, by developing new tests that would
measure the emotional reactions that seem to be so important
in determining whether a trainer uses or discards an adult dog.
In this connection, the testers have since modified the Ear
Sensitivity test (one that already had a high predictive value)
by scoring the puppy's reaction to the sound of a starting

pistol.

The second major line of research concerned the heritability of the test scores and the effects on them of selecting high scoring animals as breeding stock. Some of the sub-tests, particularly Fetch and Come, showed reasonably high heritability. Selection should have resulted in improvement in those scored, and the average figures over the years did show such improvement.

The hypothesis that there had been relaxation in standards of grading was considered but rejected on the ground that certain scores, especially that of the Sit test, which is one of those most independent of the rest, did not show such changes. The over-all change over five 3-year periods amounted to 1.2 points on a six-point scale, or approximately 25 percent, certain scores showing more change than others.

It was disappointing that the change in puppy test scores was accompanied by relatively little change in trainer success. There was some indication of a slow rise between the years 1950-58, but there was also an unexplained dip in trainer success during the years 1959-61. Since this affected both donated dogs and those bred for the purpose, it is probable that there was some loss of efficiency among the trainers, possibly because of a turnover in personnel, but there is no way of verifying what actually did happen.

The research also points up the fact that, in addition to improving the hereditary capacities of the puppies, there are at least three possibilities for improving the percentages of successfully trained dogs: 1) maintaining and improving the performance of the trainers (future research might be devoted to analyzing differences in methods used by individual trainers as well as improving the methods themselves), 2) improving the environment and training of the puppies during the period between their early life in the kennel and their final training as adults, and--unexpectedly--3) the improvement of the maternal environment. In spite of the fact that the mothers spend only a few weeks with their puppies and have no direct connection with either the puppy testing or any subsequent outside experience, there are indications that the maternal environment does have important effects, particularly in emotional reactions. The nature of these effects is at present unknown, and until these are discovered it will be difficult to determine which mothers provide the best environment for their offspring.

Finally, and irrespective of their value in predicting future performance and facilitating the improvement of breeding stock, the puppy tests are valuable as a socializing experience that brings the puppy into contact with a variety of people in situations outside the kennels. While this research did not attempt to measure these effects, since all puppies went through the same program, all our other research with dogs (Scott, Stewart & DeGhett, 1974) on the effects of early experience supports this conclusion.

References

Fishman, J. A. A note on Jenkins' "improved method for tetrachoric r". Psychometrika, 1956, 21, 305.

Gower, J. C. Variance component estimation for unbalanced hierarchical classification. Biometrics, 1962, 18, 537-542.

Jenkins, W. L. An improved method for tetrachoric r. Psychometrika, 1955, 20, 253-258.

Scott, J. P. & Fuller, J. L. Genetics and the Social Behavior of the Dog. Chicago: University of Chicago Press, 1965.

Scott, J. P., Stewart, J. M., and DeGhett, V. J. Critical periods in the organization of systems. Developmental Psychobiology, 1974, 7, 489-514.

Willingham, W. W. Predicting success in graduate education. Science, 1974, 183, 273-278.

Yates, Allen. Private communication, 1967.

HOME EXPERIENCE AND FINAL TRAINING*

Clarence J. Pfaffenberger

The Guide Dog Puppy's Life In A 4-H Club
Member's Home

Within one week after the guide dog puppy has finished
the tests given by the Volunteer Puppy Testers at San Rafael,
he is delivered by station wagon to the home of a 4-H boy or
girl in California, Oregon, Washington, Nevada or Utah. Here
he will remain until he is ready to be professionally trained
as a guide dog by the staff of instructors back at the Guide
Dogs for the Blind school at San Rafael.

From the time he was 6 weeks of age the puppy has had the
attention of the puppy testers every Thursday: the sixth and
seventh weeks for five minutes only, and thereafter for about
one half hour on each of the subsequent five Thursdays. During
this time he has lived first with his mother and litter mates
for two weeks and then only with his litter mates. In addition,
he has had visual and auditory contact with many other dogs in
the surrounding kennel areas. His canine socialization has
thus continued up to thirteen weeks of age in a constant fashion. His human socialization, which is to help him to become
a part of a man-dog team, has taken place only on Thursdays
when he has been a part of the activities in the puppy tests.

When he leaves the station wagon at the 4-H Club member
home the puppy comes equipped with a flat leather collar on
which is a metal plate engraved with three things: his regis-
ter number, "Guide Dogs for the Blind, Inc.," and the school's
phone number. To the collar is then attached a six foot fabric
leash, which has been made by a volunteer group of 4-H Club

---

*The system of care and training is described as it was carried
out during the years when this study was made.

sewing classes. The puppy raiser is also supplied with five
pounds of the same kind of dog food the puppy has been eating
in the kennel, so that his digestion will not be upset by too
rapid a change in diet. There is also bone meal, Vionate (a
vitamin supplement), and cod liver oil.

Following the instructions which he has read in the Puppy
Manual, the puppy raiser first takes the puppy on the leash to
the place in the yard which he wants the puppy to become accustomed to using for his toilet. The youngster stays there with
the puppy on leash until it has relieved itself. His previous
training for "heel on leash" has prepared the puppy for following. Without fail, the puppy takes to the idea of going with
his new master or mistress. It is remarkable that even though
all of his brothers and sisters are still in the station wagon,
once the pup has a master or mistress of his own, he seems to
lose all interest in his own canine family and is ready to become a part of his new human family.

Without the puppy tests, or some similar exercises, this
would not be true, and here it becomes evident for the first
time how important those seven weeks of socialization with
people has been to this young dog. He has learned to enjoy,
if not actually need, human companionship.

Because puppies with full stomachs are inclined to become
car sick, all puppies leave the kennels at San Rafael without
breakfast and without a drink. They are not fed enroute unless they are kenneled over night (as is necessary on the longer trips), when they are fed at night, but not the next morning. They occasionally get a small drink enroute and more at
the destination. This system has proved to be so satisfactory
that the puppies not only travel clean and dry, but rarely
have any bad effect from the trip. Even the change of drink-
ing water in their new home seems to have little bad effect,
if the puppy is brought to his new home fairly empty and not
over-fed or over-watered the first day after his arrival.

If this is the first puppy that this 4-H member has taken
to raise he is shown exactly how the puppy is accustomed to
being heeled, (a little in front of the handler), how the puppy has been trained to sit, come, and fetch, and how the sig-
nals are made and the commands given.

The puppy raiser will have prepared a bed in his room for the puppy according to the manual. Because a puppy must be thoroughly housebroken to be useful as a guide dog and be accustomed to sleeping by his master's or mistress' bed, the housebreaking begins now.

Naturally, a puppy should not be required to stay on his bed all the time, but it is unsatisfactory for him to be roaming at will either in the house or outside, both because of dangers to property which the puppy has not yet learned to respect and because of dangers to the life of the pup. Therefore, an outside dog-run has been prepared according to the manual. This run is used to give the puppy time and room to move about by himself out of the danger of getting into mischief, and out of the way of the members of the family who are busy with their own affairs.

The puppy raiser will give the puppy 15 minutes a day training in the heel, sit, come, and fetch exercises at home. Once a week the puppy and his raiser will take part in a half hour training class conducted in each county by the Guide Dogs for the Blind liaison representative, usually a 4-H guide dog puppy project leader, chosen because of his or her interest in and ability to teach children how to raise and successfully train puppies. How successful the child is with the puppy at the weekly training class is somewhat predicated on how seriously the daily 15 minute lessons have been taken. The puppy run also contributes a great deal to the success of the home training. A puppy who has had his freedom in the house or yard all day, especially if he has his own toys with which to play, has one desire when his master comes home from school. That desire is to romp. The puppy who has spent the last hour before his master's homecoming in his run is anxious to be taken out and his attention for the 15 minute training period can be gotten by the youngster without too much trouble. After the lesson they have the romp and, after that, the puppy gets his evening meal. Two meals a day are routine by this age.

There are three high points in the life of most of the Guide Dog puppies and their 4-H puppy raisers. These are: the day the puppy comes to live in the new home; the first Thursday in August, which is Guide Dogs for the Blind 4-H Field Day; and the day that the puppy, now a grown and very thoroughly educated guide dog, graduates with his blind master or mistress at San Rafael. Meanwhile, the puppy and his raiser have a systematic program to follow, but one that includes a lot of rewarding fun and excitement.

Besides the daily training program, every boy or girl comes to the weekly class conducted by the liaison representative to work his puppy in the four basic lessons: heel, sit, come, and fetch. Many of the puppy raisers do such a good job, not only with these four exercises but with those of stand, sit stay, down stay, heel free, and come free, that their exhibition at Field Day is superior to most of the exhibitions put on at regular obedience trials. This has been made very evident by several puppy raisers who entered their guide dog puppies in regular obedience trials and attained Companion Dog titles before they were returned for training at one year of age. The high scores obtained by these dogs were the more remarkable in that some of their training is penalized because of its difference from standard obedience trial requirements. A guide dog, for example, must heel slightly in front of the handler's knee, rather than behind it, and when he stops, instead of sitting immediately, he must go around the handler in back and sit by his left knee. This is done so that the dog will pull when he trains for a guide dog and also so that he will never stop in front of a blind person and give rise to a chance of tripping.

In recent years, the emphasis on obedience training has been reduced. Obedience trials as practiced at dog shows place great emphasis on inhibitory training, and the trainers found that some puppies had been overtrained to the point that they could not be easily taught to take an active partnership with a blind person. Children are now encouraged to give only a moderate amount of obedience training, consistent with life in a home and a future career as a guide dog.

Function of the Liaison Representative. The original volunteers who formed the nucleus for the present liaison representatives came mostly from dog experts in the various counties who had been county chairmen for the Dogs for Defense regional

office of which Mr. Pfaffenberger was the Regional Director
and Mrs. Heller one of the most active chairmen. This purely
volunteer organization had procured dogs which were used by the
armed forces in World War II from dog owners at no expense to
the government. Having been so involved in helping in the useful service of dogs, they gladly responded to helping in another service now that the previous one was being phased out. In
several counties the enthusiasm was so great the first year
that classes were formed to teach the children to obedience
train their puppies. These dogs were shown at county fairs and
dog shows in Napa, Humboldt, and San Joaquin Counties. Other
counties became interested and wanted puppies.

Today liaison representatives have well organized programs
in most of the counties in California, and the Farm Advisors
find them to be the sort of leaders who are best suited for
this type of a 4-H program. The fact that most 4-H programs
start in the autumn and end in the summer does not affect the
puppy raising group who continue from one year to the next,
often with puppies of a number of different ages in the weekly
training classes. 4-H Club members who are waiting for their
first puppies often attend the classes to learn what they will
have to do when the puppy arrives.

The liaison system has proved of exceptional value to both
Guide Dogs for the Blind and for the Farm Advisors as it provides a family consultant not only after the puppy arrives, but
before. Each family is visited by a liaison representative,
and the entire program is discussed. It is made clear to the
family that the expenses are expected to be about $10.00 a
month, that there will be some damage done by a young puppy,
but that this can be kept to a minimum if the rules laid down
in the manual are followed. It is made clear that the 4-H puppy raiser is expected to housebreak the puppy from the start
and that the bed for the puppy beside his or her bed is one of
the essentials for accomplishing this. That an outdoor run
will aid not only in housebreaking, but in training and in
avoiding property destruction by the puppy is also emphasized.

The liaison representative is the leader for the county
4-H Club organization for the puppy program. He or she is also
the one who is always available as advisor to the puppy raiser,

the Farm Advisor, and Guide Dogs for the Blind. In addition
to this, plus the regular weekly training classes for puppies
and puppy raisers, and the gas and tires which he burns in his
service, a quarterly report on the progress of each 4-H puppy
raiser in his care is made. This was found to be one of the
most valuable contributions and, particularly in the later reports, was strongly predictive of the success or failure of the
puppy as a guide dog (see Table 5.5). Also, since dogs, like
people, are not uniformly mature at a given age, the judgement
of the liaison representative on this point is one that could
be used profitably by the Guide Dog school. Because of the
close contact with these young dogs there is no one who is better informed of their development and potentials.

Value of the 4-H program. The puppy raising program of
Guide Dogs was at that time unique in its voluntary nature,
which had no close parallel in any of the programs in other
Guide Dog schools or any other organization for rearing dogs
in the world. At Guide Dogs, the original puppy testers, puppy
raisers, and liaison representatives, were all volunteers. At
Morristown, N. J., Seeing Eye, Inc., had its own 4-H program
but made a financial arrangement to pay the raiser's expenses
in raising the pup. In England, Guide Dogs for the Blind Association placed its puppies in homes and paid what it calls "Puppy Walkers" to follow certain prescribed feeding and exercise
formulae. Neither had the early socialization or puppy testing program, nor used the early critical period approach in the
way that it was done at Guide Dogs, and each paid, more or less,
for the services given. So far as we have been able to determine, these were the two programs that were the most similar to
that at San Rafael during the years when this research project
was going on. Since then, other guide dog organizations in
the United States have adopted similar programs.

The 4-H youngster, who could be hoping to make a profit
on a beef, pork, lamb, poultry or some other farm project, not
only gives as much or more of his time to his puppy project as
he would give to a financially profitable one, but is out of
pocket an average of $100.00 a puppy for food, veterinarian
expenses, bed, run, and grooming equipment. In addition there

are the gas and tire expenses on the family car for the trips
to the weekly training class, to the annual field day, and to
the graduation ceremony. Surveys by both the University of
California Extension Service 4-H Leaders and by a member of the
Board of Directors of Guide Dogs for the Blind, Inc., have verified that the average amount spent by the 4-H puppy raiser on
each puppy exceeded $100.00. This cost has risen in recent
years because of inflation.

The liaison representative, also a volunteer, gives his or
her time, car expense and often her home once a week with attendant refreshments and entertainment. He or she usually ac-
companies any and all members from his or her group to San Rafael for graduation of the dogs they have raised. Ironically,
while all of a litter may arrive in a county on the same day
and be assigned to members of the same county class or raisers,
it is just possible that each will be graduated with a member
of a different class and thus stretch the graduations over a
five to seven month period. No one has yet tried to estimate
what it costs to be a volunteer liaison representative.

With the number of puppies in 4-H homes sometimes reaching
200 in one year, it becomes clear that the amount annually contributed in monetary costs to this philanthropic organization
may well be considerably more than $20,000.00 by the puppy rai-
sers alone, plus whatever the liaison representatives contribute. This is a sizable contribution by one group, most of whom
are from 10 to 18 years of age. It may even pose a new question for those who are worrying about "what is happening to
our teenagers?"

Aside from the financial help which these remarkable young
people contribute to the welfare of blind people, the greatest
gift they make is in the loving care and selfless devotion they
give to the puppy raising program. It is not that they train
dogs to become guide dogs per se, but they do teach the puppies
to learn and keep them from developing bad habits on their own.
They keep alive the human-canine team spirit which was gener-
ated first at six weeks when the puppy was taken from the mother and its littermates to have a five minute socialization period with a puppy tester and to learn that it can be an individual and can associate with a human being on a high level. The

dignity that gives a person ability to develop his potential
is needed just as much by his canine partner, and the 4-H boy
and girl develop a rapport with the puppy which allows this
dignity to develop.

This is done so well that all puppies raised at Guide Dogs
for the Blind are raised by 4-H children exclusively. In the
latter years of this study, all the dogs trained at Guide Dogs
for the Blind were from their own breeding stock and all were
4-H raised by the children, except that occasionally, a liaison
representative could not resist becoming a part of the puppy
raising group and took a puppy to raise on his own. But, although he may do an excellent job of teaching, he is seldom as
successful at the actual training as the children he instructs.
Other adults as puppy raisers have a sorry record. There may
be other groups of youngsters who could do a good job, but 4-H
Club members seem to be the ideal group, and there would certainly never be any idea of changing at San Rafael.

Aside from its benefits to the Guide Dog program, a significant fact is that superior groups of teenagers give much and
achieve famously. At home, at Field Day, and especially at the
graduation of the dogs they have raised, when they present them
to the new masters as a part of the monthly graduation ceremony,
these are Americans of whom to be proud.

The Guide Dog School

The first part of the puppy's life, that of rearing and
testing at the kennels in San Rafael, takes approximately 3
months. Seven to 12 months later, after training and experience in 4-H homes, the puppy returns to the kennel and begins
the final phase of his training, which will last 5 months or
more.

There are three classes of students at the Guide Dog
School:

1. Apprentice instructors, who receive three years training at the school before they are eligible to take the California State Board examination to become licensed guide dog
trainers and instructors for blind people.

2. The puppies, which have been especially bred by the school and raised in the homes of 4-H Club members to provide the finest dogs possible. At approximately 12 months of age they receive four months or more of professional training to lead the blind. This instruction is given by the licensed instructors and, under their supervision, by apprentice instructors.

3. The blind persons, who have been accepted as students to learn to use a guide dog. At the time this was written, the maximum capacity at San Rafael was 12 students. Usually this was filled and had been each month for more than a year. The state law required that a licensed instructor be in charge of the blind people in a class 24 hours every day that they are in class. The class period was a full four weeks.

The apprentice instructor must have had at least one year of experience working with dogs to apply at Guide Dogs for the Blind, Inc. He must meet the following requirements during or prior to this training.

Academic requirements: Bachelor's Degree with a major in Education, Biological Science, Psychology or Sociology. Paid employment in some field of work with blind people, or with some other physically handicapped people, may be substituted for part of the educational requirement.

Physical requirements: No visual impairment that is not correctible to 20/20, with no visual field deficiency or evidence of pathology. Hearing 20/10.

Applicant shall be male;* between ages of 21 and 30 years; of good moral character, with a demonstrated aptitude for work with dogs, the ability to meet demands of emotional stresses realistically, and the desire and ability to apply the knowledge acquired through this apprenticeship training to the service of the blind people.

Tenure of training: A minimum of four years and not less than 8,576 hours. The first 500 hours of the apprenticeship shall be considered a probationary period.

---

*This legal requirement has been eliminated, and the organization now employs both female and male trainers. At the time this research was done, all apprentices and trainers were males.

Apprentice training curriculum. Lectures, films, discussions of techniques and a required reading program covering the subjects and techniques of teaching a dog to guide the blind and the blind to accept the guide as his able assistant make up the curriculum. Much of the training is done by using the teaching techniques of "learning while doing". Each student is required to complete the following program:

Kennel work	12 months
Under blindfold as an active participant in a current class with dog	1 month
Psychology of the dog. Theory of training.	3 months
Basic obedience training for a guide dog	3 months
Breeding and research	3 months
Public relations	3 months
In-field follow-up service	2 months
Guide dog training	12 months
Psychology of the blind	6 months
Instruction in guide dog laws and regulations and the service available to blind people	2 months
Handling and instructing of blind people, under direct supervision, not less than 22 man-dog units	6 months

During the first six months of apprenticeship, and preferably during the first three months, the student instructor becomes an actual part of the current class of blind people and wears a blindfold from the time he gets up in the morning until he retires at night. He goes through the same instructions as the other members of the class and is trained for the full month with a dog, doing all his work under blindfold. This helps to develop in him a keen sense of appreciation of the students' problems and the emotional stresses that each of them experiences. During this month he resides at the school and sleeps in a student room as a roommate of a blind student, eats with the class and does not leave the school at any time except as a student would do.

The faculty of the training school for Guide Dog Instructors is drawn from a group of five executives, each of whom is a licensed guide dog trainer and instructor of the blind and can contribute from his particular field to the education of the apprentice. Apprentice classes are usually four or more persons.

The practical application of training dogs to lead blind people under the close and constant supervision of a licensed trainer, usually either the Director of Training or the Senior Instructor, is used to teach the apprentice the correct method of guide dog training. The number of dogs trained and available for the blind students is also increased by this teaching technique.

The year or more of previous practical dog training that most apprentices have had is usually "obedience training" or "dog show exhibition". Many have had training experience with war dogs in one or another branch of the Armed Services. A few have had specialized training such as that of teaching hunting and field trial dogs or sheepherding trial dogs.

No matter in what other field the apprentice has had his experience in dog training, he will not, before now, have had the following lessons to teach his dog:

1. To walk slightly ahead of the handler and pull on the harness. (Other types of training teach a dog to walk directly beside the handler with his head at the handler's knee or, in some cases, behind the handler when not at work.) If a dog has been taught either of these methods of heeling the job of teaching him to guide by pulling on the harness is difficult and sometimes impossible. (During the nine months the puppy is in a 4-H home he is always encouraged to lead out ahead of the child handler.)

2. To come to the right side of the handler and circle behind and then sit on the handler's left with his head near the handler's knee. (Other training practices have the dog stop and sit directly in front of the handler when being called. The dog then remains there until he is told to come to heel

when he either goes behind or in front, as he has been taught, to the handler's left side.) A dog stopping in front of a blind person is likely to trip him and confuse him. A guide dog should always report to the master's left side by going behind him without stopping.

3. To pick up any object that may be dropped by the blind master and bring it to him by circling behind and sitting at his left knee and holding the object in its mouth. (Most retrieving is done only after the handler has asked a dog to "Fetch".) Like all of us, blind people may be unaware that they have dropped something, and since they do not have sight to check for themselves, the guide dog must do it for them.

4. To recognize danger and take responsibility. In all other training of dogs to serve mankind the dog is expected to respond only to the permission and will of the handler. Guide dogs have to make decisions, and the blind master must accept these decisions. When there is an open manhole, a low overhang, bad pavement, an open trench, or traffic danger the guide dog must realize that it is not safe for his master and refuse to obey any command that would endanger him. This <u>ability</u> and <u>willingness</u> to <u>take the responsibility</u> of <u>disobedience</u> to serve safely is a prime requisite for all guide dogs.

While one year of practical dog training may seem to the uninitiated to be adequate education in that field, it can actually be a big handicap to the apprentice not taken in hand at once by a thoroughly informed faculty member and carefully directed into the channels where it can be revised to be useful in educating guide dogs.

The apprentice instructor may become an asset to the school while learning. He can train as many as four dogs under supervision as compared to the complete string of ten dogs of a licensed instructor. Or, both working together, may train a single string of 14. Thus, he is not a complete loss to the program, but can produce enough to justify his salary while he learns. Toward the end of his three years of apprentice instruction, he begins to learn to work with the blind students and to teach them to use the dogs he trains, but here again only under constant supervision of a licensed instructor.

In kennel care, the apprentices, as well as the licensed

instructors, feed and groom their own strings of dogs in training. Each also cleans his own dogs' runs, takes the dogs out
to relieve themselves, and checks on the bowel and bladder reactions to be sure that the food is agreeing with the dogs and
that they are in good health. Over weekends the apprentices
take turns with the licensed instructors in dog and kennel care.
One man takes care of his own and three instructor's strings
one weekend while others take care of his on three other weekends. This is a part of the regular routine for all training
staff.

When the apprentice arrives at a place in his training
where he is qualified to instruct blind students with their
dogs, but still under the direct scrutiny of the training director or other licensed instructor, he lives at the school
for the full four-week class-period and takes the full responsibility for his part of the class, usually four students, whom
he teaches to use the dogs he has trained. This means four
weeks of 24-hour a day duty. There must always be a licensed
instructor present day and night with the blind student. This
is a state law, and the apprentice teaches his class in conjunc-
tion with the licensed instructor and lives at the school, being available at any time, day or night, that they may need
help.

The puppies. Since Guide Dogs for the Blind, Inc. breeds
and raises all its dogs from stock which has been carefully selected for more than 20 years[*], it is the purpose of the breeding and placement department to try to have available for training approximately the right number of 12 to 13 month old dogs
ready to be brought in from the 4-H homes for training each
month. Several factors may upset such calculations, because
they must be made nearly two years in advance and there is no
way of knowing definitely what training needs will be.

Sometimes very desirable applicants for positions as apprentice trainers are available at a time when new men would
not be employed normally, but because of their ability and
future value to the school a place is made for them. Four new

---

[*]In recent years, the institution has also made extensive use
of donated dogs.

apprentice trainers means that at least sixteen additional dogs
are needed for instruction. This can mean that dogs who are
less than 12 months of age will be needed. Then at the time
they would have been 12 months of age there will be additional
shortages, compounded by the number of trainers and the lesser
number of dogs left in the 4-H homes for future call-ups. Such
a shortage takes at least 18 months to remedy.

There are other problems, such as bitches failing to con-
ceive, bitches failing to come in season at their normal time,
and such unfortunate things as some parasitic disease such as
coccidiosis being picked up from poultry in a brood bitch's
foster home. This can cause the loss of an entire litter and,
if not caught at once, it can spread to other brood bitches and
their litters. Any disease or organic weakness which causes
the failure of a litter to be born or its loss once born, has
a very upsetting effect on the supply of dogs for training.

For all these reasons, breeding plans must allow for extra
matings and, hopefully, extra puppies to be raised in 4-H homes
to take up the slack. Like all plans, such calculations are
not always adequate. When they are not, younger dogs have to
be brought into training until more dogs can be produced, and
all the dogs who have been in training have to be looked over
carefully to see if a few months more training will make a safe
guide of a dog that had previously been considered too hard to
train to justify further work. Sometimes the change from one
instructor to another will have such a good effect that a dog
that seems not to be suited to be a guide dog will respond very
well and become a good one. The younger dogs down to 11 months
of age will usually do very well, but dogs younger than 11
months usually have to be faster developers than normal in order to train satisfactorily.

When dogs are needed for training, which is every four
weeks, the instructor who is to train them goes to the 4-H
homes and assembles his string. If he is a licensed instructor
he will usually bring in ten dogs. From these he expects to
train eight that will be assigned to his class of blind people
when ready. This gives him a chance to choose the eight dogs
best suited for the particular student he gets. Twenty years
earlier the instructors at Guide Dogs started with 20 dogs and

were lucky to have five who would be suitable for the class.
More often they would have only three or four. Ten years earlier the number a trainer started with was 14. Better instructors and much better dogs have made the difference, so that today ten may be started with good hopes of having eight satisfactory, although the average figures for success are somewhat
less (approximately two-thirds). In an unusually good string
there may even be good ones left for another trainer to use.
If so, they will be assigned to another trainer or an apprentice trainer for incorporating into the string which he is training. Sometimes when a trainer is short of the eight dogs he
needs for a class, extra dogs from the other trainers play a
very important part in helping him turn out a satisfactory
string. The schedule is set up at least fifteen months ahead
for the instructors, and each one knows when each of his three
classes will come during the following fifteen months.

Assembling of the dogs from the 4-H homes by the instructors who train them has great advantages and is practiced as
far as possible. This gives the instructor an opportunity to
see the dog in the environment where he has been raised, and to
visit with the family and learn of any of the dog's experiences
and peculiarities which may be helpful to him in training the
dog. He can also ascertain if the dog has actually been attend-
ing the 4-H puppy training classes that he is supposed to have
attended, and if the dog is thoroughly housebroken. It is also
important to know if the dog has a tendency to try to escape
when left alone in a kennel. This knowledge may save a dog's
life. When a dog comes from a 4-H home where he has slept beside the puppy raiser's bed for nine months and is thoroughly
house broken, he meets a severe test, because for the four
months while being trained professionally he will be in a kennel among other dogs in training, and there will be no one to
take him out to relieve himself except at certain regular hours.
His good training in the 4-H home which has encouraged a dog's
natural cleanness will usually be enough to influence him to
keep his kennel clean and wait until the regular relief hours.

It is rarely found that the 4-H puppy raiser has not
taught this habit of cleanliness, and most dogs keep their kennels clean. Some few dogs never adjust to this routine and

cannot be issued as guides because they would be a very big problem for the blind owner.

Dogs that become panicky and try to escape when they are left alone or those that develop a tension that causes them to become destructive are also never usable. Both dirty dogs and tense dogs are usually the fault of the home puppy raiser, because the proper precautions could usually have prevented either of these conditions. For this reason it is important for the person who is to train the dog to know, if he can find out, whether the dog has been allowed to develop either of these bad habits in the home. This makes the pick-up by the man who is to train the dog more important than it might seem.

Until 1955 most dogs were picked up by having them shipped to the school by Railway Express. Even the puppies were often shipped by the same carrier. The current practice of delivery of the puppies by station wagon and the pick-up of the dogs by the instructor in a training vehicle has eliminated unnecessary emotional stresses at times of great change in the lives of the dogs and has proven to be a very good investment.

At the end of four months, if the dog has advanced properly, he will become a part of the class and move into the school to live with his blind master and begin a lifetime of guiding. House breaking and stability when left alone now become very important assets to the dog and a convenience to the instructor and his students.

During the nine months the puppy is normally in the 4-H home it has learned to be accepted as an important part of the human family, to show respect for the family's property, to travel to class, to town, and often through places of more or less confusion and excitement, such as local bus stations, airports and downtown stores. The puppy has had 15 minutes a day obedience training under a special program which fits the training to the work it will do as a guide dog and works once a week in the local class for 4-H puppy training. It has learned to learn, be a good member of human society, and to feel comfortable about being with many different people and different dogs. There has been no effort by the 4-H puppy raiser to train the puppy in guide work, but basic obedience and living a useful life with people has been observed from the time the puppy

arrived at 13 weeks of age. If it is convenient to teach a puppy to handle stock or to hunt properly or do other valuable
services for the family, (except that of acting as a guard dog),
such training is encouraged by the school for, like a human, a
dog that has learned to do certain useful things learns to do
other things more readily. But a dog that has learned to guard
as a puppy will almost always become too possessive of his master and his belongings and thus become dangerous to use on public streets and in public buildings.

When the young dogs have been returned to San Rafael they
are checked carefully for any physical defects such as eroded
or yellow teeth, crooked ears, or other defects which would
make them have such a poor appearance that their blind master
might not be proud of them. Any such defect is sufficient reason to reject the dog. These faults may have not been evident
when the puppy was taken to the 4-H home. (Often they are detected while in the home, in which case the 4-H puppy raiser is
supplied with another puppy, and the defective one is taken in
to Guide Dogs to be placed with someone waiting for a pet.)

Both the instructor and a veterinarian check every incom-
ing dog for any illness and parasites. If healthy, the dog is
housed in the reception center where each shares a stall with
another dog during training. In the stall the dog has fresh
water at all times. In winter the kennel is radiantly heated,
and there is a central drainage system to provide proper clean-
ing of every stall with hot water daily and steam when necessary.

At regular intervals the dogs are all released from this
kennel into concrete floored large runs on each side of the
kennel. These runs have solid concrete walls 1½ meters high.
Thirty to forty of the year-old dogs, most of whom have never
known each other before, are released together in each of these
runs. At least one of the instructors goes out into this arena
with the young dogs to be sure that no disturbance occurs, but
he seldom sees even a raised ruff, which reflects the quality
of the stock and also the results of home living and good care
that the 4-H children have given them. In this run the dog now
learns to relieve himself in a new environment at specified
hours: the first thing in the morning, at noon, and after class
in the evening. To encourage these habits of cleanliness each

dog is fed at noon. These times will be similar to the hours
at which a blind person would want to feed his dog and take it
out to let it relieve itself. Thus, this training sets a pattern for a full four months before the blind person must take
the full responsibility for it. Any dog who fails to show that
it can be perfectly clean under these arrangements is eliminated before it is issued to a blind student. Nothing can be more
disgusting and discouraging than a dirty dog.

Both the apprentice instructor and the dogs are brought
along in the dog training courses together until the apprentice
is capable of doing most of his work satisfactorily under supervision, when he starts to train his abreviated string. Basic
obedience as it applies directly to leading blind people is now
perfected. The willingness and skill of immediately picking
up anything that is dropped and bringing it to the left side
of his master and, after alerting his master, hand it to him,
is one of the yard lessons that must be taught with great pat-
ience and skill. Teaching the dog to pull on the harness at a
steady gait of three miles an hour is started in the school
grounds and soon is extended to the residential streets of San
Rafael. Here is taught the stopping at the sidewalk curb and
the turning in the proper direction upon command by hand and
voice, such as "right" or "left". The guide dog must always
stop at a curb in time for the blind person to feel with his
foot for the curb and to decide whether he wishes to continue
another block in that direction or whether he wants his dog to
turn and take him either to the right or the left. If he is to
go in the direction where there is another curb to be negotiat-
ed, the dog must stop again, sit beside the master and await
his command, "forward". When the instructor or the student has
felt the curb with his foot and has given the command "forward"
the dog must learn to take his handler off the curb and directly straight across the street, stopping before stepping up on
the second curb, so that the person can determine when he has
crossed the street, and not trip over an unexpected obstacle.

While the dog is being trained at Guide Dogs for the Blind,
Inc., in San Rafael, it is also taught to avoid overhanging objects such as low awnings, limbs, or clotheslines and to avoid
holes and depressions which may be dangerous to his charge. It

is at such times that the dog must learn (and the apprentice
instructor also learn) that these lessons must be letter perfect, for a dog that fails in any of these or fails to avoid
dangerous traffic becomes a dangerous dog and can never be
trusted to lead a blind person.

The principal commands that are taught are: "sit", "down",
"come", "fetch", "forward", "left", "right", and "stay". There
are other words such as "hup up" which are used to encourage a
dog to walk faster. The word "no" is usually so well taught
in the 4-H home that the dog obeys it without special training.

When basic obedience has been taught and the dog becomes
accustomed to leading out correctly, the instructor and the
apprentice move with their dogs into residential San Rafael.
After a week or so in this area they move to the business district of the same city. From here the progress is across the
Golden Gate Bridge to San Francisco. The residential area and
district business areas are worked first, and from them the dogs
are gradually advanced to work on the busy downtown streets:
Market, Powell, Van Ness and even Grant (China Town). On these
streets and avenues the dogs, and the apprentice instructors,
too, learn how to adjust to heavy traffic.

Once a dog is properly trained, the instructor-trainer who
is to be responsible for the class to which this dog is to be
issued takes the dog into the heavy city traffic and into all
kinds of situations which might present problems to a blind
person with a dog. Here the instructor must work each dog in
his string satisfactorily under blindfold under the directions
of one of the faculty such as the Executive Director, the Director of Apprentice Training or the Senior Instructor. Often two
or more of these faculty members observe and score the dog and
the instructor. This is done to make sure that the dog is now
safe to lead a blind person. Special attention is taken when
the dog is directed into moving traffic to see if he will take
responsibility. The same applies in areas where construction
is going on or where the sidewalks are barricaded or cluttered.
Every instructor must be willing to trust his life to the judgement of each dog in his string before it can be approved to lead
a student.

Blind students. The students arrive at Guide Dogs for the Blind, Inc., as a complete class on a Sunday. They often come by air and are met at the airport by their instructor. Others are brought by auto by their family or friends.

When they arrive at the school they are assigned to rooms, and each is introduced to his or her roommate. They get their regular meals, but are given most of their time to adjust to their new environment and new fellow students, and no attempt is made to start teaching them until Monday.

Regular hours are kept, and on Monday everyone is expected to be up, dressed and ready for breakfast. After breakfast all assemble in a large room which serves both as a day room and a lecture room. Here each student finds the seat that suits him best, and he will usually occupy that seat at class session for the next four weeks.

There are no dogs in the class on Monday or Tuesday. The instructors not only teach the class but act as the dog for each of the students. This has several merits. One is that the instructor can talk and tell the student what he has done wrong and encourage him when he does a thing correctly. It also avoids having an untaught person confuse a trained dog by giving the wrong commands.

The first thing for a student to learn is how the leash feels and how it can be shortened or lengthened for different uses. Then he learns how the harness feels, which part is the handle which he will hold, which parts are fitted to the dog, and how it is put on the dog.

But the very important thing for the student to learn is the vocabulary that he will use in communicating with his dog and what to expect the dog to do when these words are used correctly. In teaching this the instructor works on the other end of the leash for "come", "sit", "down", "fetch", and even "heel". He also works on the dog's end of the harness for "forward", "right", "left", "hup-up", and such commands. The student is given a lesson in how a dog stops at a curb, what he is supposed to do when the dog stops, and how he is to tell the dog that he is ready to proceed or to make a turn. Practically everything that a blind person must learn to expect of his dog and every way in which he must communicate is taught by the instructors

during the first two days in class. On Wednesdays of the first
week a review is held in the morning to be sure that each student has fully comprehended (as far as one can while working
with a person) what he is expected to do with his dog. By noon
everyone is tense, because right after lunch each student, one
at a time, will come to the classroom and there will be presented with his dog.

The first Wednesday afternoon is packed with emotion. Many
a student has said when at last the cold nose nudged him, "I
never thought this could happen to me!" or "Why, he seems to
know me and accepts me right away."

As a student is seated alone in the classroom, the instructor who is to teach him for the next four weeks brings the dog
he has chosen as best suited for this particular man or woman.
He has given a small lump of hamburger to the student to attract
the dog's attention and has told the student to hold this in
his palm, hand open, and when the dog takes the food, to stroke
him and attach the leash, which he has had since Monday, to the
dog's collar. Once the dog and student have made friends they
are escorted to the student's room and given the remainder of
the day to get acquainted.

At dinner time all of the students bring their dogs on
leash to the large table in the dining room and each is taught
how to cause his dog to lie down under the table at the student's feet and so not interfere with anyone else at the table.
Any fuss among these dogs is almost unheard of.

On Thursday the student starts to work with his dog instead of his instructor, but his instructor is always right
there to help the dog and student get their behavior coordinated.

After a few days the students are ready to go into the residential district of San Rafael. Like the apprentice trainers
and the dogs in training that we have already described, blind
students progress from residential to business districts in San
Rafael, then do the same in San Francisco, then to all the harder traffic conditions of the busiest streets in this city. They
learn to get on and off busses, street cars, cable cars, to pass
through revolving doors and out again, to go up and down long
stairways, and even to walk among the pigeons feeding in the
parks, a place where it is most difficult for a dog to maintain

self-control.

There comes a time when each student must demonstrate that he can leave the Guide Dogs' vehicle, find his way several blocks away, and return completely on his own. The students all get a chance to walk across the Golden Gate Bridge and to feel the size of the cables that support it. Often a fog horn sounds beneath their feet as they and their dogs walk along with 45 mile an hour traffic on one side while on the other sighted people watch the great ships from all over the world come and go.

The students even have a trip to Muir Woods, where they walk on narrow dirt paths among the natural redwood and bay trees and often squeeze with their dogs between close growing giant trunks, left that way for the joy of the sighted, but the blind folks enjoy this, too, and feel the foliage and bark of the trees, even trying to judge the size of them by putting their arms around the trunks and then walking around until someone tells them they are back where they started.

After four weeks of daily work and instruction the class members have not only learned how to do things but have confidence in themselves and their dogs so that they have no fear about going anywhere that a sighted person can go. With a good guide dog they are actually safer in traffic than the average sighted person.

On the last Saturday at Guide Dogs there is a graduation program. The 4-H puppy raiser comes to the school to present the dog he or she raised to the blind person, who now becomes the dog's master or mistress. The dog is the diploma for the blind student. The 4-H puppy raiser has achieved a wonderful thing and usually leaves with a new puppy if he has not already received one.

One 4-H puppy raiser raised eight Guide Dog puppies, was Junior Leader with the largest number of dogs in her county, and since graduation from the University is now Home Advisor for 4-H members in another county. One of the boys took up dog training as a career and then applied to be an apprentice. He has been a licensed trainer for several years and is an important part of the faculty at the school.

All the dogs, equipment, the training, and the board and

room are given without any charge to the student or to any person or organization. Guide Dogs for the Blind, Inc., San Rafael, California, is not supported in any way by either the state or federal government. The school is a private philanthropy supported by memberships and donations or memorials and monies willed to the organization by persons who wish to have their estates used to help those who need the help of a responsible guide dog.

Once a student has graduated with his dog from the school he is taken to the airport or is met by his family to be taken home. His dog rides by his side. All public transportation organizations cooperate 100 per cent in aiding blind passengers and welcome the dogs.

If problems arise after a student has been graduated, the school has a follow-up service which will help him with any problems. Usually, the instructor who taught him at the school will go to his home and help him solve the problem. If it is necessary, the student may be brought back to San Rafael. There have been times when it was found that the student had to have a different dog. Such failures to adjust are very rare. The point is that the school intends never to allow any bad situation to develop. Every precaution is taken, even at considerable expense, to correct any situation which may seem to be headed toward failure. Social service is thus an integral part of the school work.

EFFECTS OF EXPERIENCE IN 4-H FOSTER HOMES

J. P. Scott and S. W. Bielfelt

The experience of a puppy in the Guide Dog program is high-ly standardized up until he is 12 weeks old.[*] Each puppy gets the same routine care in the kennels and is put through the same testing program. Differences in performance during this period should therefore largely reflect differences in hered-ity--individual differences within strains, strain differences within breeds, and finally breed differences. Similarly, exper-ience in the interval between 12 weeks and one year in the 4-H homes is standardized as far as possible, but there are inevit-ably certain differences in these homes: the size of the fam-ily, its location in a rural, semi-rural, or urban district, and the skill of the child as a puppy raiser. If these differ-ences have any significant effect on the final performance of the adult dogs in their training as guides, then we should get different proportions of successful dogs according to the type of home experience. With this in mind, a series of report sheets and questionnaires was prepared for the use of the puppy raisers and liaison representatives.

As part of his work in the 4-H project the child hands in a record concerning the amount of time he spends training the puppy and furnishes answers to questions concerning the puppy's habits. The first questions concern the number of training classes attended and the amount of training given the puppy at home. Then there are a series of questions involving the emo-tional habits of the puppy, followed by a question concerning its experience with frightening objects. Another group of ques-

---

[*]The period in the kennels has now been shortened to 10 weeks.

tions concerns the habits of elimination, and success in housebreaking. Then there is a section on physical defects and disease, part of which concerns symptoms which might reflect hip
dysplasia. The final series of questions concerns the kind of
environment with which the dog has had experience, ending with
one concerning the feeding habits of the animal.

These reports were collected and analyzed for all puppies
whelped in the years 1959 to 1964, inclusive. This covers a
period two years longer than the liaison representative's reports, and includes a population of approximately 600 animals.
Not every question was answered by every child, with the result
that the total number of replies varied from question to question. For example, in answer to the question "Is your dog distracted by other animals?" there were 427 answers, whereas 606
children answered the question "Is your dog friendly in the
home?"

Analyzing the results of the questionnaires presents two
problems. One is statistical in nature, determining whether
the results could be obtained purely by chance. This problem
can be solved by Chi-square analysis, since most of the questions are answered by yes or no, and these answers can be compared against the dog's later performance. Sample sizes are
large enough in this data that performance differences of 7 or
8% are usually statistically significant at the 5% level; that
is, if 62% of the dogs having a particular experience became
guides, and of those that lacked this experience, only 54% were
successful, there is only one chance in 20 that the result was
due to pure chance.

From the viewpoint of practical performance, bettering the
final output of guide dogs depends on the number of animals
that have the unfavorable experience. If only 25% of the dogs
have an unfavorable experience, improving their performance by
8% would affect only two dogs in a hundred, whereas if 75% of
the animals were involved, improvement would produce 6 additional dogs in a hundred, an important advance considering the time
and expense which goes into the final training of a dog.

The second problem is that of translating these results
into practical recommendations, which has to be done with considerable caution. In some cases the way in which a dog was

treated may be the result of the way he acted, rather than the reverse. For example, dogs which were allowed to run free did better as guide dogs, but it is possible that dogs that were allowed to run free were allowed to do this because they were well-adjusted and could be trusted. If this is true, freedom for all dogs might not result in any improvement. Consequently, using these data for modifying the 4-H program should be done with considerable caution and only where there is some clear-cut theoretical reason for supposing the effect to be a true one.

Results of the Child's Report

Emotional habits. The answers to questions concerning the dog's friendliness towards strangers, men, women, and children are in the expected direction; that is, fewer of the dogs that were reported unfriendly became guides (Table 5.1). However, the numbers of unfriendly puppies are so small that none of the results reach statistical significance. Only the answers to the question of whether the dog has bitten anyone are in the opposite direction of what would be expected, but since the difference was not great and only 22 dogs did this, the result is probably a matter of chance.

On the other hand, the answers relating to distraction are not only in the expected direction but are statistically significant, highly so in the case of distraction by dogs, and somewhat less so with respect to cats. Of the 247 puppies that were distracted by other dogs only 47% became guides, whereas 70% of the 198 that were not so distracted were successful in training. The ability of a guide dog to keep his attention on the business of guiding the person is a very important factor in successful training, and those dogs that are distracted by passing dogs or cats cannot be trusted. In this respect the reports of the child are an important predictor of training success.

An animal that fights other dogs would, a priori, be expected to be a poor risk, but only a small number ever did this, and the percentages are no different from the others. Similarly, there were only a few dogs which had ever killed another

Table 5.1

EMOTIONAL HABITS

	Question	Answer	Percent Guides	Number of Answers
1.	Friendly toward-strangers:	Yes	55	433
		No	40	25
	men:	Yes	55	417
		No	41	22
	women:	Yes	55	430
		No	33	12
	children:	Yes	55	429
		No	33	12
	Friendly-- at home:	Yes	54	475
		No	50	6
	visiting:	Yes	55	458
		No	43	14
	Bitten-- anyone:	Yes	69	22
		No	54	454
2.	Distracted by-- dogs:	Yes	47**	247
		No	70	198
	cats:	Yes	50*	254
		No	61	175
	chickens:	Yes	53	93
		No	59	231
	other animals:	Yes	55	119
		No	59	218
	Fights-- other dogs:	Yes	56	43
		No	54	425
	Killed-- another animal:	Yes	48	48
		No	55	427

animal, roughly 10% of the total, and while these did somewhat poorly compared to the rest, the figures are not significant.

The reports concerning undesirable habits such as barking, chewing, jumping on people, and being noisy or destructive when left alone, are all in the predicted direction, but the differences in percentages are small and none of them significant.

(Table 5.1 Continued)

Question	Answer	Percent Guides	Number of Answers
3. Much unnecessary barking:	Yes	49	81
	No	55	389
chewing:	Yes	49	150
	No	55	311
jumping on people:	Yes	52	133
	No	55	327
When left alone-- noisy:	Yes	51	97
	No	55	358
destructive:	Yes	50	82
	No	55	296
4. Has run away:	Yes	56	63
	No	53	411
often:		85	7
occasionally:		54	54
never:		53	408
Gone long time:		44	18
few minutes:		58	43
never:		53	408

*Significant at <.05 level
**Significant at <.01 level

A relatively small number of the puppies had ever run away, and of these an even smaller number, 18 or so, had ever run away for a long time. Of these the percentage of success was only 44%, but again the numbers are too small to be statistically reliable.

Eating and elimination. It would be expected that those dogs who were regular eaters and well house-broken would succeed better as guides, and the percentages in Table 5.2 conform to this prediction, although none of the results are statistically significant. The only one which approaches significance is that of the comparison between puppies that never relieved themselves indoors as opposed to those which did this sometimes or regularly.

Table 5.2

EATING AND ELIMINATION

Question	Answer	Percent Guides	Number of Answers
1. Regular appetite	Yes	52	414
	No	40	52
2. Relieves self indoors	Regularly	39	13
	Sometimes	52	321
	Never	61	140
3. Relieves self outdoors	Never	33	3
	Sometimes	50	8
	Regularly	54	465
4. Usually relieves self	In run	54	355
	On leash	47	116

Physical defects and disease. We would expect that such defects would be related to rejections of the puppy for physical reasons, and this is indeed the case (Table 5.3). One of the most important physical defects is that of hip dysplasia. A dog that is painfully limping cannot make a good guide dog. Of 586 puppies included in the most complete sample, 48, or 8% of the total, were rejected because of physical malformation, compared to 38% that were rejected because of emotional reasons. 2% of the animals died or were rejected for other reasons. 44% became guides, and 8% were retained for breeding stock, making a total of 52% that were desirable animals. More detailed analyses of the reasons for loss and rejection are given in another chapter. At any rate, the percentage of physical rejects among those animals noticed limping is twice as great as among those which did not limp, a highly significant figure.

As might be expected, those animals that limped had a lower percentage of overall success as guide dogs. Just the contrary result was noticed with respect to other disease conditions. This was particularly noticeable in the case of dogs having skin trouble, of which 66% became guides as opposed to 49% in puppies for which no skin trouble was reported. The results are highly significant, and it is interesting to speculate on the possible cause. One explanation is simply that

Table 5.3

PHYSICAL DEFECTS AND DISEASE

Question	Answer	Guides and Behavioral Rejects		Physical Rejects	
		Percent Guides	Number of Answers	Number of Answers	Percent of Total
1. Seen limping	Yes	50	150	26	15
	No	56	286	20	7
2. Skin trouble	Yes	66**	128	13	9
	No	49	327	34	9
3. Ear trouble	Yes	60	53	4	7
	No	53	382	44	10
4. Eye trouble	Yes	64	39	5	11
	No	52	392	40	9

**Significant at < .01 level

eczema is not always easy to detect and may have been noticed by children who were paying more attention to their pets; i.e., the "good" puppy raisers. A more interesting possibility is that eczema may be the result of emotional strain and that it is more likely to appear in dogs which are more attentive to their masters and anxious to please them. The extra attention, care, and visits to the veterinary might also have had an influence on success. Finally, there is the possibility that it is simply the result of some exposure to physical conditions which are associated with other experience favorable to success. The answers can only be obtained by further research.

Effects of experience (Table 5.4). Almost all the dogs were frequently taken into the house, and the results were no different with those who were brought in less frequently. Similarly, almost all dogs were frequently taken for rides in the car. Those that did not have this experience did slightly poorer as guides, as might have been expected, but the results are not statistically significant.

On the other hand, two kinds of experience appear to be definitely important. Puppies that were frequently taken for

Table 5.4

EXPERIENCE

Question	Answers		Percent Guides	Number of Answers
1. Dog in house:	Frequently		54	433
	Never, seldom, occasionally		54	43
2. Taken for walks in town:	Frequently		61*	114
	Never, seldom, occasionally		51	363
3. Taken for rides in car:	Frequently		55	403
	Never, seldom, occasionally		48	75
4. Allowed to run free on ranch:	Frequently or occasionally		64**	132
	Only when supervised		55	244
	Seldom or never		38	78
5. Experienced fright of:	Cars or farm machinery	Yes	54	72
		No	54	399
	Loud noises	Yes	47	83
		No	56	354
	Other animals	Yes	47	53
		No	55	376
	Bicycles	Yes	44	16
		No	55	406
	Other things	Yes	51	70
		No	55	314
6. Kind of training:	Obedience		60	20
	Class		54	347
	Home		47	60

*Significant at < .05
**Significant at < .01

walks in town did about 10% better than those that never had
this experience or had it only occasionally. The difference is
statistically significant. Even more important is the experience of being allowed to run free on the ranch. Dogs that
were allowed to do this frequently or occasionally had a 64%
chance of becoming guides; those who were allowed to do this

only when supervised had a 55% chance, or very close to the average of the whole group; while those who seldom or never had the experience sank to a 38% chance of success. The numbers are large in all groups, and the result is highly significant. As we stated earlier, one possibility is that the children only allowed superior dogs to run free. However, it is also possible to suppose that a puppy which had some experience of complete independence and meeting various problems on his own, might better develop the confidence necessary as a guide dog, especially since guide dogs, as do no other pets, sometimes have to take responsibility without help or in the face of contrary orders from their masters.

Two other kinds of experience were recorded in these questions. One was the experience of being frightened. While there were low numbers in this category, the results are generally in the expected direction; that is, animals that were frightened had a poorer chance of becoming guide dogs. This would be true whether the explanation was that the experience of being frightened carried over into later life, or that these animals simply represented those who were genetically more susceptible to being frightened. The only exception was fear of cars or farm machinery, in which there was no difference between those who were frightened and those who were not.

The final kind of experience reported concerned the kind of training given the puppy. The results are again in the expected direction, although statistically nonsignificant. Puppies given formal obedience training did slightly better than those trained in the classes, and these in turn did better than those trained only at home. It is quite possible that those puppies given obedience training were those that the raisers thought had some chance of success in competition, and hence represent a selected group. In any case, the results are not much better than puppies trained in the regular classes, and the results support the soundness of the general training program in the 4-H group. More recent experience indicates that puppies given formal obedience training become overly inhibited for work as guide dogs, and this part of the program has been de-emphasized.

Conclusions. The questionnaire was devised on the basis of experience, and the answers generally support the expectation derived from experience; that is, friendly animals with good emotional habits and having little experience of fear do better. However, in most cases the conditions of rearing were so standardized that relatively few animals, usually 10% or less, had the unfavorable kind of experience or attitude. The results of most of these experiences and habits were not sufficiently great to be statistically significant.

On the other hand, the answers to the questions concerning illness brought out the fact that the effects of severe hip dysplasia are seen early, and it would be well to have any animal that is found limping examined clinically and discarded early if found to be suffering from serious hip disorders. As we said above, the experience with skin disease is curious and deserves further research. Except in extreme cases, its occurrence is obviously not a ground for discarding a puppy before training. Finally, there are two important practical findings. Those puppies that are not distracted by other dogs have a much better chance to succeed as guides. This may be simply a genetically determined tendency that should be selected against, or it may be possible that certain kinds of training or experience can reduce or magnify this tendency in a young puppy. Finally, it appears to be highly beneficial for a dog to have the experience of running free on a ranch, probably because this helps build up the confidence of the dog in a variety of situations.

In assessing the practical value of these results, a great deal depends on the number of animals that show variation in experience. As stated earlier, if only 10% of the puppies are involved, and they do 10% poorer than the average, changing the situation would produce only 1% improvement in the total. On the other hand, if 55% of the dogs are involved and the difference is 23%, as in the case of dog-distracted puppies, an improvement might result in a 13% change in the total, which would be very important. Of course, it should be recognized that these percentage figures are estimates, and not completely exact. Even more important might be a change in allowing dogs to run free, as only about a third of the puppies were given the most favorable kind of experience, that of being allowed to run free on a ranch.

The Liaison Representatives' Reports

These reports were sent in at three-month intervals and cover the puppies born in the four years 1961 through 1964, inclusive. Except for the years 1959-60, they cover the same time period as the child's reports. Only those puppies that were trained and either passed as guide dogs or were rejected for emotional reasons are included in the analysis. Out of a total population of 445 animals, approximately 310 were trained. For these puppies not every questionnaire was completed in all details, with the result that the number of answers varies slightly from question to question. Also, in these four years, a considerable number of puppies were called in for training before 12 months of age; thus the sample size was reduced by more than one-half at 12 months. The dogs were called in for training without selection, taking the oldest puppies first, which should not have affected the proportion of animals becoming guides. However, there is a change in the percentages of animals succeeding as guides. Approximately 60% of animals rated at 6 and 9 months succeeded but only 54% of those that remained at one year. There may have been some accidental or purposeful selection of the better animals in this sample. (The numbers of future guides were reduced proportionally more than were the figures for failures.) It is also possible that animals called in earlier either performed better because of their age or were given additional training because of the scarcity of puppies and so had a better chance to succeed. These possibilities will be considered later in a different analysis. In any case, it is difficult to compare the results at 12 months with the earlier figures.

The questions fall into four groups, arranged according to subject matter. The first group includes ratings and information on the child's ability and behavior (Table 5.5). The second (Table 5.6) covers the child's home and family background. The last two groups concern the puppy himself--his training and

Table 5.5

LIAISON REPRESENTATIVES' RATINGS OF CHILDREN'S ABILITY
AND PERFORMANCE, IN RELATION TO PUPPIES' SUCCESS IN
FINAL TRAINING

Rating	6-Mo. Report		9-Mo. Report		12-Mo. Report	
	Percent Guides	No. of Answers	Percent Guides	No. of Answers	Percent Guides	No. of Answers
Very poor to fair raiser	46*	33	47	30	35	20
Good to excellent	59	278	62	274	57	125
Poor or fair trainer	54	89	56	81	42*	43
Good trainer	59	218	64	204	60	98
Incapable or doubtful	59	29	61	41	45	29
Capable	58	275	60	249	56	113
Groomed irregularly or never	63	85	66	91	49	53
Regularly	55	218	58	205	57	90
Child's attitude,						
Attentive	66	79	61	66	65	40
Interested	63	115	67	93	63	52
Enthusiastic	62	112	60	93	52	40
Excellent	57	148	58	156	58	67
All children	57	303	61	292	54	142

*Significant at <.05

experience, and the liaison representative's rating of the puppy.

Influence of the child's ability and behavior. The answers to the question concerning the child's rating as a puppy raiser show that the puppies raised by a child who was rated good to excellent as a puppy raiser succeeded in higher percentages, starting at a difference of 13%, increasing to 15% at 9 months and 22% at 12 months. Ratings of the child as a trainer were associated with similar but smaller differences in puppy performance, the differences being 5%, 8%, and 18% respectively for the three reports. Finally, the answers to the question concerning the capability of the child showed no differences except on the last report, presumably because the liaison representative was rating the puppy on what he thought the child could do rather than what the puppy actually did. While these results conform to the expectation that a dog raised by a highly rated child should perform better, they are statistically significant in only two cases.

Class attendance had very little effect on the outcome and results are omitted from the table. Practically all the children attended class regularly. The number of classes attended was, if anything, slightly greater in those children whose dogs became rejects.

At first glance, the answers to the question concerning whether or not the child regularly groomed the dog, appeared to favor by about 8% those dogs which were not groomed. However, this trend was reversed at 12 months, and it is probable that the results were simply a matter of chance.

The liaison representative's ratings of the child's attitude in class are interesting. One question refered to positive attitudes, and those children who were reported to be attentive or interested had dogs who did consistently better than the average, while those whose attitudes were rated enthusiastic or excellent had dogs that were either only average or slightly below average in performance. However, the results are only on the edge of statistical significance. The numbers of children given negative ratings were so small that no conclusions can be drawn, although the results of their dogs were in the expected direction of being somewhat below the average. It would appear that either an over-enthusiastic or a poor attitude may lead to poor performance; i.e., either trying too hard or not trying hard enough.

In general, the most important item in this group is the

Table 5.6

HOME AND FAMILY BACKGROUND; REACTIONS AND RATINGS OF PUPPY

Rating	6-Mo. Report		9-Mo. Report		12-Mo. Report	
	Percent Guides	No. of Answers	Percent Guides	No. of Answers	Percent Guides	No. of Answers
Working Mothers:						
Full-time	62	37	61	33	59	22
Part-time	44	46	49	37	53	17
No Time	59	200	63	194	55	94
All Children	57	290	61	281	55	139
Dislikes or tolerates grooming:	59	59	57	60	31**	29
Likes grooming:	58	237	61	227	59	110
Very poor to fair:	47	55	54	56	34*	32
Good Puppy:	60	251	63	240	59	110

*Significant at < .05
**Significant at < .01

liaison representative's rating of the child as a puppy raiser. This could have been affected by the nature of the dog, since the behavior of a dog that was turning out well might have been attributed to the raising given by the child alone, ignoring individual differences in the puppies themselves, but since the ratings are consistent, beginning with the earliest ratings, we can conclude that a child who consistently takes good care of his puppy has considerable effect on the outcome.

Child's home and family background (Table 5.6). Only a very small number of homes were rated as providing poor conditions for the puppy project, so that no definite conclusions can be drawn. Out of 24 dogs raised in homes rated very poor to fair, 13 succeeded as guide dogs, which is very close to the average of the group. There is no indication that home conditions as observed by the liaison representative had any adverse effect on the puppy.

Similarly there is very little variation in the question concerning the parents' attitudes, presumably because parents would not have allowed the project in the first place if they had been antagonistic. Only one father was reported to dislike a puppy, and only 10 did not encourage the child. The numbers were very similar with respect to the mother.

It had been expected that a working mother might provide a poor environment. The numbers are small in each category, but are consistent from one rating to the next. The dogs raised in homes where the mother worked full time did better than the average, those in homes with a part-time working mother did more poorly than the average, and dogs raised in homes where the mother did not work came out almost exactly on the average. It would be interesting to speculate as to why part-time work has a bad effect on the dog whereas full-time work seems to help, but since the results are not statistically significant, we can safely conclude only that a working mother has no deleterious effect. Finally, in this sample only one dog was raised by a child in a foster home and no conclusions can be drawn from the result. We can conclude that home conditions during the years covered by these reports were quite uniform, and that such variation as was reported had little or no effect.

Puppy training and experience. Two questions concerned the discipline of the dog and its experience outside the home. According to the liaison representatives, discipline was enforced very uniformly, with not more than 5 or 10 dogs departing from the rule. The children saw to it that the dog did not jump on people, jump on furniture, steal food, or bark incessantly; consequently no conclusions can be drawn regarding the effects of relaxed discipline. Almost all of the puppies were taken for rides on the floor of the car. Those that were taken through stores or taken to town often did not include all dogs, but animals having these experiences did not perform better than the average. These results do not agree with the reports by the children themselves, especially with respect to the effects of wider experience. The children almost undoubtedly had a better knowledge of what happened to their dogs than did their supervisors, and this probably accounts for the difference.

Puppy reactions and ratings. The results are also shown
in Table 5.6. The answers at 6 months to the question concerning whether the dog likes or dislikes grooming have no relationship to success as a guide dog, but the figures at 9 months favor the animals that liked grooming and significantly favor them
at 12 months. This would indicate a progressive change in the
dog as it becomes an adult, but would not be particularly useful as an advance predictor of success, since the difference becomes large only at the point where training is begun.

The answers to a question concerning the general reactions
of the dog do not indicate any differences in final performance.
There is a tendency to give most of the animals a favorable
rating and consequently there is no differential result. Again,
these results do not agree with those of the child's report,
where there were differential results, particularly with respect to distraction by other dogs. The liaison representatives
also tended to estimate that all dogs were good enough to continue in the program, so that there is no variation in the results. Finally, the ratings of the puppy by the liaison representatives indicate that those rated good had a better chance
of success than those rated very poor or fair, but that the difference does not become very great until the final rating at
12 months, when there is a difference of 25%. This corresponds
very closely with the estimates of the child's ability as a puppy raiser and trainer and indicates that the liaison representatives were actually rating the child on the basis of what
they saw in the pup.

In general, these reports by the liaison representatives
give less information than those given by the children, probably because the liaison representatives had relatively little
contact compared to the daily contact between a child and his
dog. In no case are there opposite results, but where the liaison reports showed little or no difference, the child's reports
sometimes show large differences. It is interesting that the
liaison representatives were able to predict the success of the
puppy with considerably better than chance success at 12 months,
just before the dogs went into training. In common with many
attempts to anticipate human future behavior, dog behavior is
most predictable immediately prior to the event.

The Retrospective Report

This was a questionnaire sent out to all persons who had raised puppies in the 4-H program, beginning with puppies born in 1946 and continuing with those born through 1964. It therefore includes the puppies that were described in the Child's and Liaison Representatives' Reports and also a large sample of puppies raised in earlier years. Approximately 80% of the questionnaires were returned, which is a very good result for this kind of data collection. The returns are especially meaningful because the questionnaire covered the years when the program had not yet been perfected and hence include much larger samples of practices that were later believed deleterious and discontinued. In many cases there are sufficiently large numbers of such replies so that some definite conclusions can be drawn regarding the injurious or beneficial nature of such practices. Also, the earlier sample includes the time period before the best results began to be obtained with the dogs, again giving an opportunity for a greater variation. In short, this survey is probably the most meaningful of any of those that were made. There is, however, one complicating factor, in that genetic selection was occurring over this rather extended time period and this may account for some of the differences seen.

1,306 questionnaires were returned on 1,268 dogs (a few dogs were cared for by more than one person). Of these dogs, 43% eventually became guides, 9% were saved for breeding, 6% died, 11% were rejected for physical defects, and 29% were rejected because of behavioral defects, mostly of an emotional nature. The fate of the remaining 2% could not be determined. Of the 910 dogs that entered training, 60% became guides and 40% were rejected for behavioral reasons. This is close to the results in the best years' performances, when approximately 2 out of 3 dogs have been successful.

Effects of age and sex. Almost twice as many girls raised puppies as did boys, but their percentage of success was slightly poorer, 59% for girls against 65% for boys. However, the difference is only 6%, and there is one chance in 10 that this difference was accidental.

Table 5.7

RESULTS ACCORDING TO
AGE AND SEX OF PUPPY RAISERS

	Boys		Girls		Total	
Age	Number Raised	Percent Guides	Number Raised	Percent Guides	Number Raised	Percent Guides
Below 10	2	50	3	100	5	80
10	21	67	27	59	48	63
11	30	67	69	64	99	65
12	47	66	89	57	136	60
13	58	67	101	66	159	66
14	52	69	94	59	146	62
15	45	69	79	53	124	59
16	30	47	71	61	101	56
17-20	18	55	60	47	78	49
Total	303	65	593	59	896	61

As seen in Table 5.7, there is an indication that the older children were less successful as puppy raisers. Boys 16 or over did less well than the average, and the decline in success apparently began at 14 in girls. Certainly, if all children 16 or over are compared with younger children, the percentage of success is significantly poorer, going down to 53%, compared to 59% or better at any of the younger ages. A disproportionately larger number of older girls raised puppies, but if these are removed from the sample, the sex difference favoring boys still remains.

Family background and experience. Family size had some effect (Table 5.8) in that puppies raised by only children had a poorer chance of success than those raised in families of two or more. There is no clear trend in larger families.

A number of questions were asked concerning the experience of the child and other siblings with dogs. If the children raised one or two puppies, their percentage of success was slightly better than the average, but if they raised three or more their performance was somewhat worse (Table 5.9). This may have been related to the fact that the older children had puppies that performed less well on the average, presumably be-

Table 5.8

SIZE OF RAISER'S FAMILY IN RELATION TO PUPPY SUCCESS

Number of Children	Number Raised	Percent Guides
1	241	54*
2	229	66
3	239	61
4	117	57
5	50	64
6	19	68
7	12	75

*$P < .05$

cause the older children were less effective trainers. Perhaps
the children became less effective trainers as they grew older
because after raising three puppies they became bored with the
process. On the other hand, having another puppy raiser in the
home had a moderately beneficial effect.

Unlike the more limited sample of children described in
the Liaison Reports, there were a substantial number of puppy
raisers who reported that the father or mother hated the dog,
or merely tolerated it (Table 5.10). Twice as many fathers as
mothers fell into this category, but in either case the percentage of successful puppies was barely more than 40%. It is possible that these negative attitudes on the part of the parents
were reactions to dogs that were adjusting poorly in the home

Table 5.9

EXPERIENCE AS A PUPPY RAISER

Total Number of Puppies Raised	Number of Reports	Percent Guides
1-2	776	62
3-8	126	51*
Total	902	61

Number of Puppy Raisers in Family		
1	733	59
2 or more	169	66

*Significant at $< .05$

Table 5.10

EFFECT OF PARENTS' ATTITUDES

		Number of Puppies	Percent Guides
Father's Attitude:	Likes	734	62
	Tolerates or hates	88	42**
Mother's Attitude:	Likes	848	62
	Tolerates or hates	44	41**

**Significant at <.01

rather than the attitudes being the cause of the dog's poor performance. Nevertheless, puppy raisers would be handicapped by
such an attitude on the part of their parents, and such a home
would be a poor risk. The Liaison Reports indicate that such
conditions did not often exist in later years, when greater personal care was taken in the selection of families and introduction of puppies into them.

Other questions concerning the family background showed
little or no effect. For example, dogs raised by Protestants
were no different from those reared by Catholics. While the
great majority of the children came from families connected
with some church, the dogs of those who reported no church con-
nections did, if anything, somewhat better than the average.

Conditions of rearing. The results are summarized in
Table 5.11. The most important of these concerns the question
of urban versus rural environment. Town and city dogs showed
no differences from each other, but they were significantly
poorer than their country cousins, averaging only 50% of success. The ranch, farm, and suburban dogs were more successful,
in that order. Most guide dogs are used in town or city conditions and hence one might expect puppies raised under these conditions to perform best, but country dogs actually do somewhat
better. However, as indicated by the other questionnaires, it
is an advantage for the country dogs to be given frequent trips
to town. This report definitely supports the policy of raising
the guide dogs in cooperation with the 4-H programs, since

Table 5.11

CONDITIONS OF REARING

Condition		Number	Percent Guides
Sleeping Place:	House or bedroom	632	61
	Porch or garage	94	71*
	Dog house or pen	97	60
	Yard	24	58
	Inside & out	51	53
Family Away During Day:	Yes	168	54*
	No	668	62
Boarding:	Often	24	38*
	Sometimes or never	749	61
Used in Hunting:	No	742	60
	Birds	62	48
	Small animals	30	80*
Other Dogs:	None	173	54
	1 or more	700	62
Family Dog is:	Kind, obedient	609	63
	Shy	21	86*
	Aggressive	61	51*

(Differences between shy and aggressive dogs significant at $<.01$)

Length of Time in Home:	6-8 months	381	64
	9-12 months	450	58
Town or Country:	Ranch	247	66
	Farm	229	62
	Suburb	242	58
	Town or city	147	50**

*Significant at $<.05$
**Significant at $<.01$

these are located predominantly in rural areas.

Other conditions of rearing show interesting results. For some unknown reason, a dog whose sleeping place is in a garage or on a porch does better than a dog sleeping elsewhere, although this may be simply a chance result. The regular absence of the family during the day decreases the percentage of success in training, as might be expected. (In the previous section, working mothers had no effect, but this would not necessarily mean that the whole family was absent). Dogs are highly

social animals. Apart from the emotional distress caused by
being left alone, dogs would be more likely to fall into bad
habits if the family were away for long periods each day. Placing the dog frequently into a boarding kennel has an even more
serious effect. While this happened to only 24 dogs, their percentage of success was less than 40%.

Not many of the dogs were used in hunting. These small
numbers give the curious result that puppies used to hunt birds
did less well than the average, while those used to hunt small
animals (presumably mammals) did significantly better. We would
expect that dogs that were trained to hunt either might suffer
from this because they later might become distracted as guide
dogs, or contrarily, might benefit from the experience of learning to act under control. With no clear theory and with only
small numbers involved, we can come to no definite conclusions.

The great majority of puppy raisers had other dogs in the
home, and their puppies did only slightly better than the average as prospective guides. On the other hand, family dogs apparently could have differential effects on the puppies. The
great majority of family dogs were reported to be kind (presumably to other dogs) and obedient (presumably to people).
Under these conditions, puppies did slightly better than the
average. On the other hand, a few family dogs were reported to
be shy, and the puppies that were raised in those families showed the highest rate of success in any category. If the family
dog was aggressive, the chances of success for the puppy were
definitely poorer. These and other results indicate that one
of the very important consequences of the experience in the 4-H
homes is the development of confidence in a variety of situations and in a variety of contacts. Here the presence of a shy
dog seems to help the puppy develop confidence, whereas an aggressive one has the opposite effect.

Keeping the puppy in the home until it is over one year of
age apparently had some detrimental effect, though not a significant one. As will be seen later in the book, there seems to
be no differential effect of the age of training within the limits of 10 to 15 months, and this result may well be a matter of
chance.

In conclusion, one of the most interesting findings in the

whole series of questions is that concerning the town and country environment. The rank order of success is perfectly correlated with the degree of rural environment to which the dog
was exposed, with the town and city dogs being on the bottom.
This agrees with the results from the other questionnaires,
which indicate that a dog that is allowed to run free on the
ranch does better than one not allowed this experience. On the
other hand, it is also important for the rural dog to be taken
on frequent walks in town, as indicated by the Child's Report.

Summary

The Child's Report includes five items that gave important
results. The first of these is distraction by other dogs, where
the rate of success was 47% versus 70% of dogs not so distracted.
This distraction affects 60% of all the dogs, so that if all of
them could be raised to the 70% level there would be 14 more
successful dogs in a hundred. However, it is doubtful that this
trait is entirely produced by training and experience, and it
might be well to introduce a test of "dog distraction" into the
early puppy tests. It would also be well to try to train the
puppies not to be distracted, if effective methods for this can
be developed.

There are two important items relating to physical disease.
Hip dysplasia shows up as limping in the young dogs, and is an
important cause of rejection for physical reasons before final
training. The possibility of genetic selection against this
trait is discussed in a later chapter. There is also the curious correlation between skin trouble and successful training.
This provides an interesting field of research concerning the
relationship between physical disease and behavior, but does
not suggest any means for practical improvement through the
rearing or selection of puppies. An obvious possibility is
that skin disease in dogs, like allergies in human beings, are
in part caused by emotional reactions; i.e., are psychosomatic.

The most important items from a practical viewpoint concern the dog's experience of being given frequent walks in town,
and being allowed to run free on a ranch. A puppy that was

taken on such walks had a 61% chance of success versus a 51% chance among those that were not. Since dogs that had this experience made up only about 25% of the population, there should be an improvement of 7-8 additional successful puppies in a hundred if all could be given this experience. Similarly, those dogs that were allowed to run free on the ranch were only about 25% of the population, but succeeded at a rate of 64% versus 55% for the others. If all had this experience, the improvement would amount to 7 dogs in a hundred.

The Liaison Report chiefly indicates that during the later years the 4-H program was working very well indeed. The liaison representatives were able to recognize good puppy raisers quite early in their experience, and this knowledge could be used in placing the puppies. However, only a very small number of children were actually poor raisers, and little improvement in the total program could be made in this way.

The most meaningful set of reports, from the viewpoint of scientific analysis, are the Retrospective Reports, because they include both larger numbers and a greater degree of variation in the way the puppies were raised. These reports indicate that younger children do better than older ones up to and including the age of 15 in boys and 13 in girls. There is an interesting correlation here with the known earlier age of puberty in girls. The more mature children are probably less interested in doing a good job with their puppies. However, since the older children included no more than 25% of the total there would be relatively little practical effect of keeping them out of the program, especially since their puppies' success rate was 53% compared to 63% for the younger children. The net gain might be at the most 2-3 dogs per hundred. Similarly, children should probably not be encouraged to raise large numbers of puppies, but only one-seventh of the total number did this and little improvement could be expected from such a change.

Negative attitudes by the parents are associated with a very poor rate of success, 40% versus 62%, but this involved only 5% of the whole population. The liaison representative's reports indicated that very few puppies got into homes like this in later years.

There were several other items that involved what appear to be strong effects, but only very small numbers of puppies. Sleeping on a porch or in a garage appeared to have a favorable effect compared to sleeping in a house or bedroom, as most of the dogs did, but without a clear theoretical reason for the effect, this probably should not be taken too seriously. It is possible that this may be connected with the apparently negative effects of a child's being over-enthusiastic. A child that is too much attached to a puppy may cause it to become more dependent, and hence less well able to change over to being a guide dog.

Dogs that were often boarded out in kennels had a success rate of 38% versus 61%, but this happened to very few of them. Obviously, the practice should continue to be discouraged. As stated above, the effects of hunting experience are unclear and need more investigation. The presence of another dog in the family can have a considerable effect, but the only practical application would be to make sure that the other dog was not aggressive, as this situation definitely reduces a puppy's chance of success. A shy dog, on the other hand, seems to have a favorable effect, rather than providing a poor example, as might be supposed.

Having the family be away during the day is associated with a success rate of 54% versus 62%, but since dogs that had this experience formed only 20% of the total, the possible improvement amounts to only two or three dogs in a hundred.

Similarly, the town or city dogs that had only a 50% success rate formed only 17% of the total, and converting all the dogs to country life would result in a gain of only 2 dogs in a hundred.

The general result is to reinforce the kind of program that is already in existence. There are not many important changes that could be made on the basis of these results. The most important, those of being given frequent walks in town and the opportunity of being allowed to run free on a ranch, amount at the most to 7 or 8 dogs per hundred. Also, we cannot assume that different dogs are involved in the answers to each question, since many of the answers to different questions may be correlated. (The research project came to an end before these correlation statistics could be done). Assuming that the answers are correlated to some extent, and also that it will never be possible to run a completely perfect program, we can estimate that changes based on the above results might result in raising the general level of success by about 10%, so that a similar sample of dogs might be performing at 70% instead of 60%. Of course, some of these changes have already been made in the course of the general improvement of the program.

From the viewpoint of general theory, we can conclude that the most successful dog is one that has a wide and frequent variety of early experience, that is raised on a ranch with freedom to roam, but is also taken on frequent controlled walks in town. It is fascinating to speculate on the possible implications for human living, especially in the light of the decline of rural population in this country. In the future, very few American children will have the experience of running free in woods and fields, and very many of them will be brought up in the more restricted environments of towns and cities. Of course, the rural child should benefit only if he has frequent experience of frequent visits to towns and cities as well. On the other hand, we can help the city child to achieve a wider capacity for adapting successfully to life by broadening his experience and at least occasionally removing him from restrictions. Our goal, as with the guide dogs, is the development of an individual who is competent, confident, and unafraid in a variety of situations.

THE HUMAN+GUIDE PARTNERSHIP

John L. Fuller

What happens to the dog that has been trained successfully and is finally assigned to a blind student? In previous chapters we have traced the process whereby the puppies are selected (or discarded) for further training, and the factors that lead to their ultimate success. As the following study shows, once the guide dog has been successfully trained he usually enters a long and stable partnership with his blind master.

The long and exacting procedure of rearing and training a guide dog reaches its culmination when the dog is assigned to a student for a four-week course of intensive training. In the majority of cases the dog is probably better prepared for this course than its human partner. The dog will be required to continue in the same behavior for which it has been specifically directed since birth, but the human partner must change established habits and acquire confidence in the guiding ability of an animal. Ideally the dog will become an extension of its human partner, serving him as a visual guide and on occasion taking responsibility for acting contrary to his orders when to obey would be hazardous. The problem of the human partner is less acute when he returns to the school for a dog to replace an incapacitated guide. Nevertheless, there is a need for mutual learning of individual habits in order to approach the ideal human+guide partnership.

During the course of the research project I was able to observe about a dozen established human+guide units working in the field. The mobility of most of these pairs was remarkable. Blind men operated small businesses and blind women managed households; students achieved fine records at universities with the aid of guide dogs. I needed no elaborate statistical analysis to confirm the value of the guide dogs for all of the indi-

viduals I visited. However, there were substantial variations
within the group in the degree to which the guide dog was actually utilized. Some retired individuals living with a spouse
or a child were relatively immobile, and gave the impression
that it was easier for them to stay inside and let other members of the household take the responsibility for outside functions. The guide dogs in such homes tended to be overweight
and seemed to have moved into the status of companion, rather
than a guide, as their human companions aged and became less
active. But if the younger individuals were included, even
this small sampling of guide dogs in the field confirmed the
value of the guide dog in helping blind people to achieve mobility, and demonstrated the essential soundness of the training program for the dogs and the selection program for students.

It was not feasible to make an extensive field-study of
the guide dogs in service over the vast area served by Guide
Dogs for the Blind, Inc. Our studies of the human+dog partnership were therefore based upon an analysis of data routinely
collected by the Social Service Department of Guide Dogs for
the Blind, supplemented by data on the dogs collected by the research project personnel. Each prospective applicant submitted
a form giving personal and family data and a description of the
reasons for wanting a guide dog. A physician's report and,
wherever possible, a home interview report by a staff member of
Guide Dogs for the Blind were also obtained. A master file of
all accepted students and of all the dogs assigned to them was
maintained as a part of the permanent records. From these
sources data for each student were entered on a service record
card for IBM computation. The items sought are listed in
Table 6.1.

During the early years, records of Guide Dogs for the
Blind, Inc. were not as complete as those kept in later periods;
hence there were gaps in the available information. Another
feature of the data was that the records of dogs issued since
1957, and some issued still earlier, were not complete since
some of these dogs were still in service at the conclusion of
the research project. Therefore, the estimates of the length
of time dogs served as guides based upon complete records show
a systematic bias, since dogs with short durations of service

Table 6.1

INFORMATION SOUGHT FOR SERVICE RECORDS

Student

1. Case number ____.

2. Number of dogs student received prior to this one, including all sources ____.

3. Identification--case number in first class ____.

4. Age at graduation ____ years.

5. Sex ____.

6. Living conditions: Single with family ____; Married with spouse ____; Living alone ____.

7. Cause of blindness: Unclassified or unknown ____; Congenital ____; Infection, poisoning ____; Trauma ____; Degenerative disease primarily ocular ____; Degenerative diseases, general ____.

8. Age at onset of blindness ____.

9. Occupation: Unknown or unclassified ____; Unemployed ____; Academic student ____; Unskilled, semi-skilled ____; Trade ____; Sales ____; Business ____; Professional ____; Housewife ____; Retired ____.

Dog

10. Identification, IBM No. ____.

11. Number of times issued prior to this time ____.

12. Breed: German Shepherd ____; Labrador Retriever ____; Chesapeake Bay Retriever ____; Golden Retriever ____; Other ____.

13. Sex ____.

14. Age at graduation ____ months.

15. Month of birth ____. 16. Year of birth ____.

17. Age at retirement ____ months. 18. Age at death ____ months.

19. Duration of association of human+dog unit ____ months.

20. Duration: Less than a year ____; 1-5 years ____; 6 or more years ____.

21. Cause of discontinuance: Unknown ____; Student incapacitated or dead ____; Student personal or social ____; Violation of contract ____; Dog incapacitated or dead ____; Behavior of the dog ____.

22. Rating by trainers ____.

are over-represented as compared with those with long service. It would have been desirable to have based conclusions upon the length of service of the older dogs, all of whom had terminated service, but the number of cases with adequate information would have been seriously reduced.

Before turning to the tabulated data which deal with quantities and which provide a basis of planning for the future based on past experience, it is of interest to consider some of the individual human+dog teams who made up the statistics. The seven case histories following were abstracted from the records with only the names of the individuals changed. They were selected to illustrate the diversity among the blind persons who use guide dogs and how these dogs serve them.

A Look at Seven Case Histories

1. Jane Miner was a 21 year old San Francisco girl living at home at the time of her application. She had been a premature baby who became blind from the excessive oxygen administered after birth. Her education was obtained at the California School for the Blind in Berkeley. She was an attractive and well-groomed girl with poise. However, she was tense and rather awkward during her training course at Guide Dogs for the Blind. She often turned into and so collided with her dog and was inclined to overcorrect. Her dog, a female German shepherd raised in Madera County, compensated well for the student's errors. With her dog Miss Miner attended a university, lived in a dormitory, and at the time this report was made she planned to major in psychology.

When she first arrived at college, she encountered difficulties because her dog was distracted by other dogs on the campus. A field session with a Guide Dogs instructor apparently enabled her to overcome this problem.

2. Jim Frank of Texas was 29 years old, a mechanic, when he became blind from retinitis. He was married and the father of one child. After his blindness he worked in a service station and as a retail clerk. At 41, after 12 years of blindness, he applied to Guide Dogs for the Blind and was accepted for training. He was an excellent student and became a part-

time representative for the school in his home state while continuing as a retail clerk. He moved to a new home on a small ranch and had excellent confidence and mobility.

3. Sherman Hayward was a California business man and rancher with three years of college education. A diabetic, he became partly blind at the age of 43 and completely blind by the time he was 45. Mr. Hayward was encouraged by his secretary to investigate Guide Dogs for the Blind, Inc., and visited the school.

He obtained some training in Braille and in the use of the abacus before finally deciding to obtain a dog for greater personal mobility. He did well in training with his female German shepherd, even though some severe insulin reactions restricted his activity during his course of training at the school. When he returned to his home and wife and two children, he operated his business and even resumed, with enthusiasm, his former hobby of horseback riding.

4. Jimmy McIntyre of Oklahoma was 45 years of age, single, and lived with his mother when he applied for his guide dog. He had lost his sight from glaucoma ten years before and had used a dog issued to him by another guide dog school. With his guide dog he had supported himself as a door-to-door salesman. His training at San Rafael with a male Labrador retriever was uneventful. The instructor felt that McIntyre was inclined to undercorrect his dog. However, the dog worked out satisfactorily and Mr. McIntyre continued to be successful with his sales work.

5. Martin Galtman of California had two dogs from Guide Dogs for the Blind, one when he was 19 years of age and the second when he was 30. The first one provided the mobility which helped him to obtain a Masters Degree in Education. He married after college and had two children. Mr. Galtman was then employed as a classroom teacher. As a hobby he did darkroom and cabinet work. During his second course at Guide Dogs for the Blind he was very helpful to the other students in his class.

6. Mrs. Jean Haynes of California had been blind since infancy because of retinal blastoma. After she obtained her first guide dog at 19 years of age, and completed one and one-half years of college, she then married, had one daughter and be-

came a housewife. When she was 27 years of age Mrs. Haynes'
dog died unexpectedly and she returned to San Rafael for a replacement. She requested a female but one suited to her was
not available, so she was given a male Labrador retriever. She
had been fearful that a second dog would never be equal to her
first guide. Despite the fact that she was accustomed to working a guide dog, this student had some problems. One of them
was the lack of firmness in correcting the dog when he became
distracted. Eventually she adjusted properly to her new dog
and he gave her good service in her home, work, and shopping.

7. <u>Mrs. Dolores St. Claire</u>, mother of one child, became
blind from diabetic retinitis at the age of 31. Two years
later she obtained her first dog from Guide Dogs for the Blind,
Inc. After seven years she returned for a replacement. Five
years later her second dog began to show aggressiveness which
she was unable to control. She returned for her third guide, a
female German shepherd. This dog proved to be very satisfactory, and Mrs. St. Claire, at 46, managed her household and
took part in her neighborhood affairs.

Men and women from college age to post-retirement make
good use of guide dogs, as these examples show. Not every
blind person, however, can use a dog. Some may be physically
or temperamentally incapable of managing their guides. The living conditions for some may be unsuitable for the use of a guide
dog. In a large measure the success of the program at San Rafael is due to the care which is taken in the selection of the
students and the careful pairing of students with dogs. The
case histories recounted here show the necessity for proper adjustment between the human+dog partners, which may continue well
after the student and his dog have been graduated and returned
home. While only a few incidents occur in which training must
be continued in the field, the fact that Guide Dogs for the
Blind, Inc. has had such service available is one of the reasons their program has been so successful.

An Analysis of the Service Records

The objective of the analysis of the service records was
to estimate the length of service of the guide dogs and the po-

ABOVE: A guide dog makes college possible. (Photo by Virginia
        Beauchamp).

BELOW: Benny Larsen, now Executive Director of Guide Dogs for
        the Blind, checks the progress of a human+guide team.

134

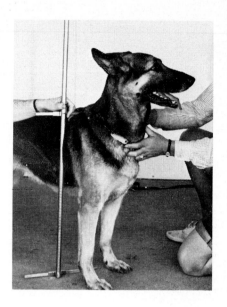

ABOVE: German shepherd
       being measured for
       Shoulder Height
       (see Chapter 7)

BELOW: With a guide,
       mobility is pos-
       sible, even on a
       busy street.
       (Photos by Virginia
       Beauchamp)

tential demand for the replacement of guides. For long-range
planning such information is essential. To accomplish this we
investigated the reasons for which human+dog units discontinued
their partnerships by dividing the causes primarily into stu-
dent-related and dog-related categories. We also looked for
factors which seem to correlate with long-lasting and succesful
partnerships. This information should be valuable for future
selection of those candidates for training who are most likely
to make the best use of guide dogs. Such judgments were regularly made, using the experience obtained over 25 years in the
selection of new students. This fact must be kept in mind when
interpreting the tables. Whether an applicant was 20 years of
age or 65, he was not accepted unless the staff believed that
he was qualified for training. Unselected samples of blind
persons might be very different from the selected samples with
which we dealt.

Who Applied for Guide Dogs?

In this study a total of 4,000 applications for guide dogs
were reviewed and pertinent data abstracted. Of these 1,068
were initial applicants to Guide Dogs for the Blind, Inc., although some of them had had dogs from other schools. The records were not always clear as to the source of the previous
guides. The information regarding an applicant and his dog at
the beginning of this partnership was usually quite complete.
Since many students did not report the time when their dog eventually became incapacitated as a guide, the time of the retirement of each dog as compared to his entering service was not as
definite. This made it necessary to assume that the dogs whose
retirement had not been reported before their death had served
until they died. In a few cases death was not reported, but it
could usually be assumed that dogs which had been issued within
the last five or six years, even if there was no recent report,
were still working. It is likely that some of the dogs unre-
ported for longer periods were still in service, as has indeed
been found to be true in a few cases.

It is interesting to note the proportion of men to women
applicants. Data available did not show whether the proportion

Table 6.2

CHARACTERIZATION OF APPLICANTS FOR THEIR FIRST GUIDES

A. <u>Age of Applicant at Initial Application</u>

Age in Years	Number of Male Applicants	Number of Female Applicants
Under 20	53	37
21-30	167	77
31-40	188	105
41-50	208	94
51-60	81	39
Over 60	8	2
Unrecorded	7	2
TOTAL	712	356

B. <u>Age at Onset of Blindness</u>

Age in Years	Number of Male Applicants	Number of Female Applicants
Under 1 year	71	88
2-10	50	46
11-20	96	59
21-30	124	41
31-40	152	63
41-50	110	32
51-60	60	7
Unrecorded	49	20
TOTAL	712	356

is similar to the ratio of blindness among male and female citizenry, but it is known that in World War II there was only one woman in the armed services who lost her sight in line of duty as compared with a very large male population. The one woman

Table 6.3

CAUSE OF BLINDNESS AND DURATION OF HUMAN+GUIDE PARTNERSHIPS

Cause of Blindness	Numbers		Age of Dog in Completed Partnerships		
	Male	Female	N	Mean (Months)	S.D.
Congenital	23	33	12	54.8	33.7
Traumatic	250	67	185	74.9	45.4
Measles	6	8	10	48.9	38.8
Other Infections, Poisoning	44	40	46	78.6	44.0
Cataracts	43	19	31	69.1	46.5
Other degenerative ocular disease	185	97	151	67.7	40.9
Diabetes	69	35	43	64.6	39.3
Other degenerative general disease	17	10	19	71.2	47.9
Other and unknown	73	47	64	62.7	45.3
Total	710	356	561	69.7	43.6

received a guide dog at San Rafael. The applications to Guide Dogs for the Blind, Inc. showed an almost constant ratio of two males to one female in every age bracket (Table 6.2A).

As information was not complete on human+dog units still in service, only the 560 complete case histories were used to compute average length of service. The mean duration was found to be 69.7 months (5.8 years) with a standard deviation of 43.6 (3.6 years). The high standard deviation indicated that many partnerships lasted far beyond the average, some as long as ten years and even more. There was no difference in the duration of completed partnerships among the different age groups of the applicants, though the number of graduates beyond 60 years of age was too small to allow a sound test of significance.

Table 6.2B shows the age of the onset of blindness for the same applicants. Again, no significant variation in average duration of the partnership was found for any of the groups.

In Table 6.3 is a classification of the causes of blindness among initial applicants. The male:female ratio of 2:1 does not hold for all causes. Sexes are represented approximately equally in the congenital and infection-poisoning group. An excess of males predominates in the traumatic causes, indicating a much greater exposure to accidental injury. Although the numbers are small, there is a hint that partnerships involving individuals congenitally blind or those blinded by measles (probably also at an early age) were less durable than the average.

Occupation and Home Conditions of Applicants

We considered the possibility that the duration of a partnership might be related to the occupation of the human member, and attempted to classify the occupation of each applicant at time of blindness and at the time the application was made. We also summarized responses to a query on the application form concerning future plans. Replies to the last item were often omitted or difficult to classify. We found no significant variation in duration of partnerships among occupational groups. The data are summarized, however, in Table 6.4 because it is interesting to document the fact that students at Guide Dogs for the Blind, Inc. include representatives of many occupational groups.

In comparing occupations before blindness and later at application it was clear that there had been a shift from gainful employment outside the home to unemployment or housekeeping. Although the number of cases was small, the farmers appeared to have the greatest difficulty in continuing work after blindness. It was unfortunate that more information was not available concerning future plans, because this was the one category which showed a possible relationship with the duration of partnerships. Applicants who stated that they had no plans for employment or that they planned to retire had substantially shorter partnerships (30.8 and 52.5 months) than the average (69.7 months). It is plausible that an economic objective strengthens the determination of a blind person to continue the use of

Table 6.4

DISTRIBUTION OF PREVIOUS OCCUPATIONS AND
FUTURE PLANS REPORTED ON INITIAL APPLICATIONS

Occupation	Before Blindness		At Application		Future Plans	
	Male	Female	Male	Female	Male	Female
Unemployed	13	4	257	56	22	6
Student	59	37	39	21	36	17
Unskilled	152	29	99	25	54	14
Sales	165	28	112	30	160	45
Business, Professional	126	49	79	21	103	41
Farmer	35	0	10	1	11	0
Housekeeping	1	48	7	138	1	44
Retired	0	1	12	1	17	5
Unknown	69	62	80	49	304	177
Total	620	258	695	342	708	349

a guide dog, but biases in the data are also possible. This
aspect of student selection might be carefully checked in the
future.

The home environments of the applicants were surveyed for
possible relationships with the duration of human+guide partnerships. Conditions may change after a guide is acquired; in
fact, the guide may be the means of effecting a change, and the
new environment is probably more critical than environment at
application. However, selection must be based upon past history rather than an assumed future. It turned out that there
were no reliable differences among partnership durations of persons from any of the home environments. However, the summary
of replies gave further information on the composition of the
student body and are included here for their descriptive value
(See Table 6.5).

Table 6.5

HOME ENVIRONMENTS OF INITIAL APPLICANTS

Home Situation	Number of Applicants	
	Male	Female
Single, with parents	110	67
Married, with spouse	350	164
With adult children	11	17
Single, with roommate	16	12
Living alone	139	73
Institution	2	1
With adult brother or sister	21	4
Unknown	61	18
Total	710	356

The reasons which blind persons gave for wanting a guide can be almost completely summarized by one word, mobility. Some applicants, predominantly men, mentioned that mobility was concerned with their occupation. Women were more apt to refer to mobility for personal errands. Ten persons out of 1,410 applicants mentioned health as a reason for wanting a guide. Presumably they believed that the exercise of walking with a guide would be beneficial. Increased mobility and independence was obviously the common factor for all applicants and outweighed all other motives for obtaining a guide. We had thought we might distinguish among applicants by their motives, but if such differences existed they were too subtle to be extracted from a file of application forms.

The search for characteristics of students which might lead to better success with a guide dog (as measured by the duration of a human+guide partnership) was thus largely unsuccessful. This result was actually encouraging, for it confirmed the value of the criteria used by Guide Dogs for the Blind at that time in the selection of students. The problem of selec-

Table 6.6

PERCENTAGE OF DOGS IN SERVICE AT SPECIFIED AGE

	Number at Start	Age in Years			
		4	6	8	10
Males	148	70	45	23	11
Females	220	81	62	39	25

tion was in many ways more difficult than that of a college, for the applicants were neither homogenous in age nor in background. The common denominator of blindness with a strong motive for achieving independent mobility appeared to override all differences. This does not mean that all students were equally proficient with their guides. A few partnerships broke up within a year. The point is that the age of applicant, the cause of his blindness, his education, occupation, and home environment were not predictive of his success. At least they have no predictive value among a group which had already passed Guide Dogs' criteria for admission to the course.

The Guide Dog in Service

The records of 1,380 guide dogs at graduation show that 80% were between 12 and 24 months of age. Only 2% were graduated before 12 months of age; the remaining 18% were over 24 months. Age at graduation was about the same for both sexes and all breeds. Dogs older than 24 months at graduation were primarily serviceable animals which were no longer being used by their first partner, and were reassigned to a new blind person.

The percentages of dogs remaining in service at various ages are reported in Table 6.6. The tabulated data include only about one-half the potential sample, for many records were incomplete. There is no reason to suspect that any group of

Table 6.7

DURATION OF HUMAN+GUIDE PARTNERSHIPS

Sex of Dog	Total Number	Percentage per Years of Duration			
		2-3	4-5	6-8	9 plus
Male	129	27	28	30	15
Female	213	22	24	24	30

dogs was selectively lost from the sample, but early discontinuance of a partnership was probably more likely to be recorded than a later one. Hence the average age at discontinuance of a partnership is likely to be higher than that shown in the records. Length of service for the three major breeds was about the same. However, the records show a significant trend for female guides to give longer service than males.

The greater average age of females at retirement is also reflected in greater average duration of the partnerships in which the dog is a female. Expectations of the duration of a partnership for both sexes have been calculated from the available data (Table 6.7). The chances for termination at any given age bracket are approximately equal up through 8 years within each sex but females were twice as likely to serve continuously for nine years or more.

Causes of Discontinuance

In 447 instances it was possible to determine the cause for discontinuance of the human+guide partnership. These are shown in Table 6.8. The table contains few surprises, but it is worthy of mention that 25 guides were reported as dead or incapacitated within one year of graduation. There is a small bulge of behavioral failures during the first year, but even after five years some partnerships are terminated for sharpness or other fault. The number of discontinuances for personal and social reasons, including breach of contract, is small.

The trainers' ratings of the dog during the course were converted into a point scale: poor, 1; good, 2; and very good,

Table 6.8

REASONS GIVEN FOR TERMINATIONS OF HUMAN+GUIDE PARTNERSHIPS

	Duration of Partnership				Percent of Total Terminations	Average Trainer's Score
	Under 1 Year	1 to 5 Years	Over 5 Years	Unknown No. Years		
Human - physical incapacity or death	5	43	38	38	27.8	2.0
Human - personal or social problem	0	3	4	6	2.8	2.1
Contract violation	2	4	2	4	2.6	2.2
Dog - incapacity or death	25	80	158	2	59.4	1.9
Dog - behavioral problem	14	10	6	3	7.4	2.0

3. There seems to be no relationship between these ratings and causes of discontinuance. This probably means that the technical skill of the dog, which is the basis for the trainer's judgment, is so high for all guides produced by Guide Dogs for the Blind that it does not limit service. Even those dogs whose services terminated for behavioral faults had good ratings on the average. We cannot really determine from the records that these animals were poorer performers. They may have been required to work under difficult conditions, or their human partner may have been unwilling to tolerate some weakness. Some blind people (see Case History No. 7) who had trouble with one dog were happy with its replacement. Some guides which were returned by a blind person were reissued and did very well with a new partner. Empirically the trainers have learned to fit guide and person very well, but sometimes readjustment is necessary in the field.

We considered the possibility that younger students might be in better physical condition than older ones and that discontinuances in this group might be predominantly caused by the incapacity of the dog. However, we found no such trend. Regardless of the age of the applicant---up to 60 years---one-third of the partnerships ended for student-centered reasons and two-thirds for dog-centered reasons. Physical incapacity or death was the major factor in both categories of causes.

Replacement Guides

The need of many blind persons for guides extends far beyond the maximum possible service period for the canine member of the partnership. A summary of 1,408 applications showed that 344 (24%) were for replacements of previous dogs from Guide Dogs for the Blind, Inc. Of the 1,068 first-time applicants to Guide Dogs, 177 (17%) were previous recipients of dogs from other institutions. Thus past experience demonstrated that about one-third of all applications were from previous users of guide dogs. There was no reason to expect that this ratio would change greatly.

The employment characteristics of the applicants for replacement guides varied slightly from those of initial applicants. Since they were generally older, the proportion of those giving the occupation of students was somewhat less. The most significant difference was in the proportion of unemployed persons, 29% for first applicants and 14% for applicants for replacements. We interpreted this difference as an indication that a substantial proportion of blind persons had, with the aid of their guides, been able to obtain and keep employment.

Another prediction from these data is that within eight to ten years after graduation, half of the students will have returned to Guide Dogs for the Blind for a replacement. This future demand must be considered in planning the size of training facilities and the production of breeding stock.

Duration of Service and Hip Dysplasia

Hip dysplasia is a structural anomaly that involves deformity and weakness of the hip joints. It has long been of concern to dog breeders because it can contribute to lameness. Thus x-rays of the hip had been routinely taken on adult guides since 1960. These were rated on the Hage scale which ranges from zero (complete luxation with head of femur out of socket) through one (subluxation with head of femur not seated in socket but still located inside the rim of the socket) to five, an ideal joint structure. A series of 370 consecutively issued guide dogs of Guide Dogs for the Blind breeding, whose Hage ratings were known and which were issued between 1959 and 1966, were taken and analyzed for evidence of shortening of service by dysplasia. Very few retirements would be expected in this group, of course, since the average duration of service was greater than the time spanned by the observations. We were interested, however, in possible accelerated deterioration of guides because of insufficient attention to hip dysplasia.

The sample has hips that are far from the ideal. The numbers in each rating class were: (0), 10; (1), 141: (2), 81; (3), 87; (4), 29; and (5), 22. Among this group thirty guides had retired, nineteen for causes which were clearly unrelated to hip problems. Two of the remaining had been retired because of lameness. Both had ratings of (1). The nine retirees for whom no reason was given were ranked on the Hage scale as (0),

Table 6.9

NUMBER OF GUIDE DOGS WITH SPECIFIED LENGTH
OF SERVICE HAVING SPECIFIED RADIOLOGICAL
RATINGS OF HIP QUALITY

Years of Service	Hage Scale					
	0 (complete luxation)	1	2	3	4	5 (ideal)
7	0	1	1	1	3	1
6	0	2	3	7	1	2
5	3	12	11	7	0	0
4	1	21	8	12	3	4
Retired under five years	1	1	0	1	0	0
TOTAL	5	37	23	28	7	7

1; (1), 2; (2), 1; (3), 3; (4), 1; and (5), 1. The number was
too small for any definite conclusion, though the distribution
was not unlike that of the entire sample.

Greatest interest lies in considering the ratings of dogs
issued from 1959 through 1962, which had an opportunity for
four to seven years of service. What happened to guides with
substandard hips (ratings of 0, 1, or 2)? The answer is easy
to see in Table 6.9. (Guides killed or dying from disease were
excluded from the table.) Sixty-three of sixty-five guides
with 0-2 hip ratings were working; two had been retired with
less than five year's service. Among 42 guides with hip ratings of 3 to 5, 41 were in service and one was retired early.
It is evident that hip dysplasia is not a serious factor in the
guides reared by Guide Dogs for the Blind, even though their
hips may not attain accepted radiological standards. Dogs that
show obvious symptoms of lameness are eliminated at training
(see Table 5.3), but even here only 15% of puppies noticed limping were so eliminated. This record of performance raises the
question of whether it is necessary to place much emphasis upon
radiological examination of hips in the selection of breeding
stock.

Summary

Our examination of applications showed that the human members of human+guide partnerships are very diverse. No great differences between men and women of different ages or different occupations were found with respect to duration of the partnerships. About one-third of all applications were for replacement guides. Such applicants were older and less apt to be unemployed.

The three major breeds performed equally well in the field, at least as judged from statistics. The mean age at death of 454 guides was 8 years, the mean length of service 6-1/2 years. Both are actually longer by some unknown amount because of biases in the reported data. Female guides tended to have longer periods of service than males.

Death or incapacity of one or the other partner is the major cause for termination of partnerships. Hip dysplasia is not a serious cause for retirement among guides, and many guides with poor radiological ratings performed well in the field.

PHYSICAL CHARACTERISTICS

John L. Fuller

A guide dog must not only possess behavioral competence for complex tasks, but must meet physical standards. It is important that the dog and its human associate be matched in size and strength so that they work together smoothly. It is also important that the guide dog be attractive in appearance, conforming to an accepted standard of form, color and bearing. Compliments by sighted persons on the appearance of a guide dog are reported to be very important to the blind owner.

A number of body measurements were made on the dogs reared at San Rafael by the volunteer puppy trainers and the staff of Guide Dogs for the Blind. Over the years a tremendous amount of data were collected, more than is appropriate for this general account. In this chapter we have summarized some of highlights of the findings, including tables of the average physical measurements for each of the three major breeds as puppies and as adults. Such data can be useful in comparing the physical characteristics of this population with other representatives of the three breeds. In addition, we have devised a simplified set of measurements which convey most of the information provided by the more complex set actually used in the project.

General procedures. Puppies of Guide Dogs breeding were weighed weekly up to twelve weeks of age and again when they returned to the home institution for training. Each weight was recorded to the nearest tenth of a kilogram. In addition, a number of body measurements were made at eight and twelve weeks and again near the end of the training period when the animals were essentially adult. From these extensive data we have chosen certain measurements which characterize the three major breeds used as guides and which demonstrate that the stocks

changed physically over the period covered by this study, presumably as a result of selection for desirable characteristics.

Description of measurements. The following measurements
were made with a steel tape calibrated in metric units and recorded to the nearest tenth of a centimeter.
1. Muzzle lengh (Mu). Tip of nose to stop (beginning of
    forehead).
2. Over skull (OS). Front of stop to highest point of
    occipital crest (base of skull).
3. Neck length (Nk). Occipital crest to a line connecting
    points of shoulder blades.
4. Body length (BL). Shoulder points to base of tail.
5. Tail length (TL).
6. Face breadth (FB). Distance between tear duct open-
    ings.
7. Ear length (EL). Base of ear to tip.
8. Chest circumference (CC). Measured just behind the
    elbows.
Three measures were taken with anthropometric calipers.
9. Ear spacing (ES). Distance between anterior attach-
    ments of the ears. This is a measure of cranial
    breadth. Prior to 1954 the measurement was made over
    the skull with a tape so that the early and late data
    are not comparable.
10. Brisket depth (BD). Vertical distance, chest to back
    just behind the elbows.
11. Height (Ht). Floor to tip of shoulder blades when the
    dog is standing fully upright.
Puppies were weighed on an infant scale up to eight weeks,
and then on a platform balance, thus giving the final physical
measurement of:
12. Weight (Wt).
Figure 7.1 depicts the measurements in schematic fashion.

Breed comparisons. Table 7.1 presents the average adult
physical measurements of the three major breeds maintained at
Guide Dogs for the Blind during the early 1960's. All animals
whelped during 1961, 1962, and 1963 were included, plus the

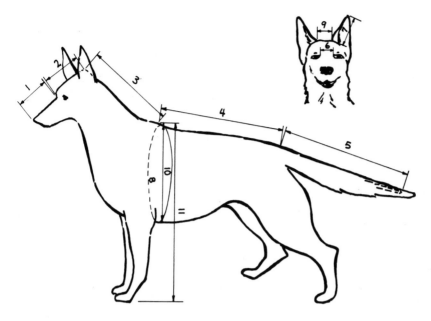

Figure 7.1.   Physical measurements.   Numbers correspond to des-
             criptions in the text.

Labrador retriever females from 1960, which were added in order
to bring this subsample up to reasonable size.

Standard deviations (SD) were computed separately for each
year. In the table we present the highest SD of the three years
in order to give an idea of the maximum variation to be expected
over a short period of time. Two-thirds of all observations
will usually fall within plus or minus one SD of the mean, and
95% will deviate less than two SD. All measurements were made
on young adults, generally between 15 and 19 months of age.

Differences among the breeds were not striking. This
should create no surprise, since all three were chosen because
they met the physical requirements for guide dogs. Overlapping
measurements were found in almost every category, as is evident
from the ratio of differences between means to the standard
deviations. We did no calculations of the statistical significance of differences between breeds, but certain differences
are obvious.

Females are three to five kilograms lighter than males on
the average. Labradors are generally lighter than goldens or
shepherds. The two retriever breeds have broader skulls and

Table 7.1

ADULT (12 TO 19 MONTHS) PHYSICAL MEASUREMENTS OF DOGS BORN IN
1961, 62, AND 63, FROM GUIDE DOG STOCK. LINEAR MEASUREMENTS
ARE GIVEN IN CM; WEIGHT IN KG. OVERALL MEANS ± HIGHEST STAND-
ARD DEVIATION IN ANY ONE YEAR

	German Shepherd		Labrador Retriever		Golden Retriever	
Muzzle length	11.2±0.7	10.5±0.7	10.4±0.7	9.5±0.5	10.2±0.6	9.5±0.7
Over skull	16.4±1.1	15.3±1.1	17.3±2.8	15.8±1.0	16.6±1.2	15.6±1.3
Neck length	22.5±2.2	21.3±2.0	20.6±2.7	18.4±2.8	21.4±2.4	19.9±2.6
Body length	58.6±3.9	55.2±3.7	52.6±3.0	51.6±4.3	55.9±4.4	53.2±3.7
Tail length	42.5±3.8	40.2±3.5	36.2±3.4	33.3±2.0	38.2±3.8	36.2±2.5
Face breadth	5.9±0.5	5.4±0.5	6.0±0.4	5.6±0.3	6.1±0.5	5.8±0.9
Ear length	12.0±1.0	11.4±0.9	13.2±1.1	12.4±0.8	13.9±0.9	13.4±1.1
Chest Circumference	74.8±2.9	69.5±4.4	70.6±3.1	68.7±4.2	73.0±3.5	70.0±3.5
Ear spacing	9.7±1.0	9.2±1.1	11.0±1.3	9.9±1.0	11.1±1.2	10.1±0.9
Brisket depth	26.6±1.5	24.4±2.0	24.7±2.1	23.8±1.9	25.4±1.5	23.5±3.1
Height	62.4±2.3	54.5±3.6	56.7±3.0	52.8±2.9	57.6±2.9	55.0±2.8
Weight	30.4±4.2	25.6±4.3	27.6±3.7	24.4±3.7	30.1±3.1	26.4±3.1

shorter muzzles than the shepherds. The original shepherds
were considerably longer and taller than the retrievers, but
over the years (see below) the breeds have come closer together.

Intercorrelations of measurements. Product-moment correlations were computed between the measurements separately for each age, breed, and sex. This index can vary between +1 and -1. A correlation of zero indicates a purely random association between the two measurements of a pair; positive values indicates that an individual high in one tends to be high in the other. Negative values indicate that an individual high in one measurement is low in the second. A study of the complete data indicated that corresponding correlations in males and females of the same breed were very similar. The correlations for the two retriever breeds were also much alike, as were corresponding sets of data for eight and twelve weeks of age. Therefore, the computations as a whole are well illustrated by the tables for German shepherd and Labrador retriever males based on measurements at eight weeks and as adults (Tables 7.2 and 7.3). Correlations falling between 0.15 and -0.15, the range in which statistical significance is questionable, are replaced in these tables by an asterisk.

The order in which the variables were arranged places the highest correlations for each measure along the main diagonal, as nearly as possible. The purpose of this ordering was to detect a simplex (Guttman & Guttman, 1965), an arrangement of correlations in which the size of the coefficients would decrease regularly moving away from the diagonal along each row and column. For example, if we take standing height (HT) in Figure 7.2 and start at the diagonal and move to the right, the correlations read 62, 46, 49, 30, 31, 20, which is reasonably close to a descending order, but not perfect. Simplex patterns like these are based upon the rank order rather than the absolute size of correlations, and are thus different from factors derived from factor analysis. It was impossible to arrange all twelve measures in a simplex, from which we conclude that more than one independent process operates to produce differences in conformation. Nevertheless, if we look at the table again and focus on height, we see that most of the measures of head size are grouped at the left, while on the right are two measures of overall size and then three measures of length (omitting the one head measurement which is out of place).

Simplexes can be formed from smaller numbers of selected variables which apply to all breeds at all ages, and one of

Table 7.2

INTERCORRELATIONS OF PHYSICAL MEASURES IN GERMAN SHEPHERD MALES AT EIGHT WEEKS OF AGE (LEFT OF DIAGONAL AND AS ADULTS (RIGHT OF DIAGONAL). VALUES BETWEEN 0.15 AND -0.15 ARE SHOWN BY **. DECIMAL POINTS ARE OMITTED BEFORE ALL VALUES.

| | HEAD | | | | HEIGHT | | SIZE | | LENGTH | | | |
	Face Breadth	Muzzle Length	Over Skull Length	Ear Length	Brisket Depth	Standing Height	Chest Circumference	Weight	Tail Length	Head Width (ES)	Body Length	Neck Length
FB	--	97	84	75	50	31	**	**	**	**	-27	**
Mu	99	--	85	76	56	38	**	**	**	**	-25	**
OS	88	88	--	67	58	47	24	**	21	**	**	**
EL	79	80	75	--	45	38	**	**	22	**	-18	**
BD	73	75	80	72	--	64	53	40	35	26	**	**
Ht	66	70	77	73	85	--	62	46	49	30	31	20
CC	38	42	58	53	76	81	--	62	41	24	37	19
Wt	41	44	61	56	72	74	79	--	41	34	41	17
TL	37	40	53	56	65	74	74	75	--	52	42	22
ES	**	**	21	**	30	33	43	45	38	--	54	18
BL	**	**	22	**	33	43	60	64	52	72	--	**
Nk	25	27	41	41	47	52	53	54	46	33	45	--

Table 7.3

INTERCORRELATIONS OF MEASURES IN LABRADOR RETRIEVER MALES AT EIGHT WEEKS OF AGE AND AS ADULTS.
(Format and Abbreviations are the Same as Those of Table 7.2)

	HEAD				HEIGHT		SIZE		LENGTH			
	Face Breadth	Muzzle Length	Over Skull	Ear Length	Brisket Depth	Standing Height	Chest Circumference	Weight	Tail Length	Head Width (ES)	Body Length	Neck Length
FB	--	99	91	79	75	44	**	-16	33	-29	-60	**
Mu	100	--	92	81	78	51	**	**	34	-29	-62	**
OS	98	98	--	82	79	57	22	**	33	-28	-60	**
EL	88	88	91	--	71	54	18	**	37	**	-44	**
BD	95	96	96	91	--	75	54	27	31	**	-46	17
Ht	88	90	91	90	94	--	71	44	35	**	-23	28
CC	63	66	71	69	78	86	--	60	19	21	22	50
Wt	77	77	77	82	81	77	65	--	19	33	36	33
TL	81	82	81	84	86	90	86	91	--	**	**	19
ES	-26	-29	-26	**	-26	-24	-19	**	-19	--	62	23
BL	-39	-40	-31	-21	-28	-19	**	***	**	72	--	19
Nk	49	49	48	50	57	55	49	53	59	-15	**	--

Table 7.4

ELEMENTARY SIMPLEXES - PHYSICAL MEASUREMENTS

(In each matrix the values above the diagonal are for males; those below the diagonal are for females. Entries are product-moment correlation coefficients with decimal points deleted. Mu=muzzle length; Ht=standing height; TL=tail length; BL=body length. These four measurements can be used for a simplified procedure that gives almost as much information as the original 12).

	German Shepherd				Labrador Retriever				Golden Retriever			
					Eight Weeks of Age							
	Mu	Ht	TL	BL	Mu	Ht	TL	BL	Mu	Ht	TL	BL
Mu	xx	70	48	-08	xx	90	82	-41	xx	87	79	-43
Ht	70	xx	74	43	92	xx	84	-21	91	xx	78	-30
TL	39	71	xx	52	88	91	xx	-10	71	86	xx	-09
BL	-08	41	50	xx	-42	-48	-38	xx	-42	-26	-15	xx
					Adults							
Mu	xx	38	15	-25	xx	51	34	-62	xx	49	24	-72
Ht	39	xx	49	31	58	xx	35	-23	52	xx	49	-34
TL	13	48	xx	42	46	50	xx	-03	31	41	xx	-01
BL	-25	37	43	xxx	-64	-49	-24	xx	-70	-37	-18	xx

these is shown in Table 7.4. These variables were selected in the following way. Starting with skull measures, three of them-- FB (face breadth), Mu (muzzle length), and OS (over skull)-- have such high intercorrelations that any one can stand for all. Muzzle length, since it falls in the middle, was chosen to represent the group in the smaller simplex. EL (ear length) is closely associated with this group, but does not form a simplex with them in shepherds and was discarded.

ES (ear spacing), supposedly a measure of skull breadth, stands apart from other skull measures. It is either uncorrelated with them (shepherds) or negatively correlated (retrievers). The only consistent high positive correlation of ES is with BL (body length), a fact for which we have no explanation. Actually, ear spacing is compounded from both the space between

the ears and skull height and may be affected by the size of
the occipital spine and width of the cheek bones as well.

It is not unexpected to find BD (brisket depth), Ht
(height), and CC (chest circumference) highly intercorrelated
since BD contributes to both height and chest circumference.
The interdependence of these three variables makes it desirable
to choose only one, height, for further analysis. Wt is closely
associated with this group, but does not form a good simplex
with them.

Nk (neck length), BL (body length), and TL (tail length)
are longitudinal dimensions of regions of the vertebral column.
Nk shows a peculiar pattern of intercorrelations which is not
readily interpretable. TL and BL were more consistent and were
chosen along with Mu and Ht for presentation as simplexes. Table 7.4 shows that the intercorrelations of these four variables
for twelve different sets of dogs can be placed in the same order with almost perfect agreement with the rank order requirements. Insofar as the physical measurements are used to rate
general growth and to guide selection for body size, these four
dimensions plus weight should be as useful as the more complete
set. Other measurements might be added if selection should be
initiated for special conformation considered important for a
guide dog's function.

Another interesting point about these tables is that the
correlations are higher in eight week old animals than in adults,
particularly those between skull and trunk measurements. Unlike
adults, young dogs tend to be large or small all over, and head
measurements only become relatively different later. In the
Scott & Fuller (1965) data for 5 different breeds, various body
measurements, many of which were identical to those used here,
were all highly intercorrelated, indicating that dog breeds are
differentiated much more by head shape than differences in body
conformation.

Long-term changes. Yearly data for the complete set of
twelve measurements were available as follows: German shepherds, 16 years; Labrador retrievers, 15 years; and golden retrievers, 8 years. The number of individuals in some year-
classes was small so that annual fluctuations are likely to be

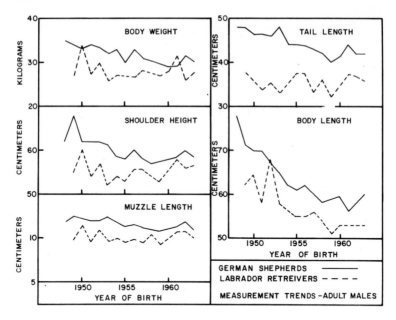

Figure 7.2. Measurement trends for adult German shepherd and Labrador retriever males over a sixteen-year period. The most pronounced change was in body length, producing a somewhat smaller and more compact dog.

large. Nevertheless, it became apparent that some highly significant changes had occurred in physical characteristics over the period studied.

A survey of all measurements showed that the five used in the general simplex were representative of the entire set. The yearly averages for adult German shepherd and Labrador retriever males are shown in Figure 7.2. Changes in the females and in the golden retrievers of both sexes were similar. Trends of the 12-week measurements were almost identical to those of the adult measurements indicating that the factors operating to produce the changes were effective early in life.

The major features of these curves can be briefly summarized. Muzzle length has dropped about 1 cm in the shepherds and has remained essentially constant in the retrievers. Shoulder height, tail length, and body length all fell significantly in shepherds, but only body length decreased in Labradors. The dates of most rapid change in the shepherds vary among the measurements. Height fell between 1949 and 1955 and has remained nearly constant since, with a possible rebound in 1962 and 1963. Length of tail fell over a longer period until about 1959 when the final level was reached. Body length appeared to decrease until 1961. Weight changes paralleled the shifts in linear dimensions.

These changes have brought the shepherds closer to the retrievers in size and conformation. The present shepherds of Guide Dogs for the Blind breeding are shorter and more compact than their ancestors, but their skulls and muzzles are only slightly changed.

A portion of the changes may be attributable to inbreeding. Correlations between inbreeding coefficients and the five physical measures of Figure 7.2 are as follows:

	Males	Females
Muzzle length	-.09	-.09
Weight	-.17	-.14
Height	-.16	-.26
Tail length	-.25	-.29
Body length	-.29	-.37

All except the correlations with muzzle length are significant at better than the .01 criterion. The greater the degree of inbreeding in a particular dog, the smaller its size measurements.

The correlations tend to be higher for those measures which have changed the most. Since some selection for size and conformation was practiced during the same period that inbreeding was increasing, it would be difficult to disentangle the relative contribution of the two types of genetic modification. Additional analyses of the data might contribute to a solution, but are beyond the scope of the present report.

Conclusions. These analyses show that the changes in physical characteristics of the dogs in this study could be effectively described by a set of five measures: muzzle length, body length, tail length, shoulder height, and weight. Over the years, selection has produced changes in these dogs, generally in the direction of a more compact, shorter bodied type of dog, and, in the case of the shepherds, a somewhat smaller animal approaching the size of the retrievers. These changes are in a direction desirable for guide dogs. Indeed, the San Rafael shepherds give a distinctly different impression from the larger, long bodied, sloping backed animals usually seen in the show ring. Selection for changes in body proportions have therefore been effective.

Continued collection of information on these characteristics could be useful in keeping track of the stability of the breeding populations. The records which were analyzed for this chapter give documentary proof of progressive changes in the physical attributes of the San Rafael guide dogs over the course of eight to fifteen years. Such measurements require little effort and can be consistently monitored by individuals responsible for a breeding program of this type.

We looked for but did not find evidence that physical measurements provide a basis for predicting the outcome of guide training and success in the field. Physical characteristics play a part in determining the usefulness of a guide dog, but they are inherited separately from trainability. This confirms the conclusion from the earlier Scott and Fuller (1965) study, that physical measurements have little effect on behavior, except where they affect it in such obvious ways as long legs making a faster runner. Among guide dogs, the principal physical requirement is that they be of size and proportion that allow the blind person to walk with them conveniently.

References

Guttman, R. & Guttman. L. A new approach to the analysis of growth patterns: the simplex structure of intercorrelations of measurements. Growth, 1965, 29, 219-232.

Scott, J. P. & Fuller, J. L. Genetics and the Social Behavior of the Dog. Chicago, University of Chicago Press, 1965.

THE GENETICS OF GUIDE DOG PRODUCTION

Benson E. Ginsburg

The physical and behavioral diversity among dogs is a
source of wonder and speculation to everyone who encounters
it. Recent finds by Dr. Bruce Howe of the University of Chicago indicate that the dog was associated with man at least
14,000 years ago, long before man had domesticated sheep and
cattle. Within this time span, all of the different breeds were
formed.

Most of this was done by persons with no scientific knowledge of heredity. Indeed, all early dog breeds were developed
in the absence of such knowledge, which did not exist in acces-
sible form until the early 1900's, when Mendel's laws were re-
discovered, verified, and applied for the first time. With the
advent of this information, it became possible to understand and
interpret what had been done, as well as to analyze problems
that are still occurring and to provide hypotheses and methods
leading to their solution.

The bases for forming a new breed are variations in size,
color, coat, leg length, tail, eye color, behavior, and many
other attributes. Each must have initially arisen by mutation
as an abrupt genetic change (Burns and Fraser, 1966; Little,
1957; Scott and Fuller, 1965; Winge, 1950). Such mutations as
were preserved formed the starting points for new breeds or
varieties.

The known histories of certain modern breeds show that a
new breed can be produced very rapidly. The basic development
of the Doberman pinscher, for example, was primarily the work
of one man, and occurred within a time span of about 20 years,
or less than 15 dog generations under favorable breeding circumstances (from 1890, when serious breeding began, to 1912, when
the breed was first officially recognized in Germany). To be

sure, many refinements occurred later, and both the preservation
and genetic improvement of all breeds is still going on. The
Airedale terrier was, similarly, a recent comer, though developed over a somewhat longer interval.

Among the three breeds commonly used at Guide Dogs for the
Blind, the origin of the golden retriever was only established
in 1952 when Lord Tweedmouth's great nephew made his great
uncle's kennel records available. The breed was created through
various crosses, beginning in 1864 with a yellow-colored dog
that appeared in a litter of flat-coated retrievers that are
normally black. Here, as in so many other cases, the desire
for the exotic manifested itself, and Lord Tweedmouth mated
this rare coat color variant with a Tweed water spaniel. He
bred some of the resulting puppies to another Tweed spaniel,
and some to black retrievers. He then line bred the progeny
until the early 1880's, introducing crosses with the Irish setter and the bloodhound along the way. Selective breeding to
establish consistency of type followed, and the golden was officially recognized as a breed in England in 1910 and by the
American Kennel Club in 1932.

Thus, a number of modern breeds were developed by a program of judicious crossing and progeny selection over a relatively short period of time. In contrast, the development of
the modern German shepherd, under the virtual control of Captain von Stephanitz from about 1899 to World War I, constitutes
an example of genetic selection within a breed. Von Stephanitz
persuaded fanciers to avoid inbreeding, insisted on careful
record keeping, and on the objective evaluation of each potential sire or dam's conformation, temperament, and trainability.
This provided useful information on each dog and permitted the
breeder to eliminate those individuals with undesirable characteristics from the breeding pool. Again, within the lifetime
of one man, a tremendous influence was exerted upon the characteristics of a breed of dog. Similarly, the development of a
special strain of shepherds as guide dogs was accomplished
within a few years.

The Genotype-Phenotype Distinction;
Dog Breeding in Practice

While it is all very well to breed from individuals who
themselves exhibit the characteristics (phenotype) desired in
their progeny, it has long been a matter of practical knowledge
that not all dogs with the same characteristics have the same
genetic potential (genotype) for passing these on to their offspring. In males, this was known as prepotency. A prepotent
sire was one whose offspring would resemble him, usually in
matings with a variety of bitches of the same breed. It was
also known that some breedings were better than others. Thus,
one sire might throw excellent puppies out of one or more
bitches and have many more inferior progeny when mated to other
bitches, even though these might be just as excellent specimens
of their breed as their counterparts. Looked at the other way
around, the same thing can be said for the bitch. Those matings
that produced outstanding results were called "nicks". When
they occurred, they were usually repeated.

Results of Genetic Analysis

Variations in Body Form: The Genetic Erector Set. Stockard and his associates at Cornell University used a completely
different approach in the analysis of the inheritance of body
type and temperament in the dog (Stockard et al., 1941). Not
only did Stockard and his associates cross different breeds,
but they crossed those that were as unlike in their attributes
as possible. Among such crosses were long- and short-nosed
dogs, long- and short-legged dogs, as well as many others that
differed widely in various physical characteristics. In general,
the first generation hybrids were well balanced dogs and showed
combinations of one or another parental attribute with intermed-
iacy. In other words, they resembled one or the other parent
with respect to some characteristics, and appeared to be some-
where in between the two parental types for others. For the
first category, it was as though the characteristics of one of
the parents made no difference, i.e., one characteristic was
dominant over the other. For the second category, it seemed as

though each parent contributed quantitatively to the characteristic in question. When these first generation progeny were crossed with each other, the results were entirely and spectacularly different. It was as though the heredity came in bits and pieces that could be recombined in all possible ways. The length of the upper jaw could be genetically dissociated from the length of the lower jaw, and badly overshot or undershot individuals could be produced in the second generation after a cross of a long-nosed breed with a short-nosed breed (Fig. 8.1). In similar fashion, leg length was independent of body size; ear size independent of head size; the fit of the skin could be tight or loose. The color of the coat and of the eye could vary. There is, therefore, tremendous genetic variation in virtually all aspects of body structure, and these variations can be reassembled in almost any imaginable combination!

Variations in Behavior. Similar variations were found for behavior in this and in other studies (see Scott and Fuller, 1965; Burns and Fraser, 1966). For example, temperament and behavior have been shown to be under genetic control in such aspects as aggressiveness, olfactory acuity, tendencies toward territoriality, the distance over which a dog will react to a command, the tendency to vocalize when hunting, the tendency to bark or to be quiet, and numerous other characteristics which man has selected in relation to the development of breeds for specialized functions.

Phenotypic Variation in Wild vs. Domestic Canids

Two aspects of dog genetics should be underscored here: one is the tremendous degree of variation, and the other is that this variation is readily expressed. This is one of the features that differentiates many domesticated forms from their wild relatives. Inbreeding within dog breeds, for example, demonstrates that there is hidden genetic variation, because characteristics are produced which are latent but not usually manifest in the parent stocks. Similarly, the results of crosses between breeds provide a dramatic illustration of both the amount of variation and its expression.

Figure 8.1. Second generation dachshund-Boston terrier hybrids showing independent variation in upper and lower jaws. Note similar variations in head, tail, and leg shapes. (After Stockard, by permission of the Wistar Institute.)

In a wild species, many of these variations would be mal-
adaptive, and wild Canids such as wolves, coyotes, and jackals
do not vary nearly as much within their respective species as
do dogs. If one inbreeds wild Canids, as we have done, there
is relatively little variation expressed. Furthermore, in first
generation hybrids between dogs and coyotes, the progeny are
unusually shy, even by comparison with the wild species. These
and similar phenomena suggest that the domestic dog has been
selected by man to preserve and exhibit as much of its genetic
variability as is biologically possible. Man cultivates the
exotic in his domestic creations. In nature, however, most
such variations would be considered freaks and would have difficulty in surviving. While there is genetic variability in
the wild, its expression is buffered. One therefore gets an
exaggeration of some of the characteristics coming in from the
side of the wild progenitor (such as shyness or wariness) as
soon as the genes having to do with these characteristics are
combined with those from the less buffered background of the
domestic species. It is, therefore, comparatively easy to sort
out various types of variability in the dog and to select for
combinations of behavioral and physical characteristics relatively rapidly, since these express themselves directly (Ginsburg, 1968, 1972, 1976).

The Domestic Dog -- Unity Across Diversities

While we have been emphasizing differences, there are also
striking similarities among all dogs. If one observes a class
in obedience, representatives of almost any breed can be seen
going through the same training procedures and giving similar
responses, although some breeds are much harder to train than
others. If one leafs through the pages of a well illustrated
dog book, one is impressed with the extent to which the beagle,
the harrier, and the English and American fox hounds resemble
one another. Although beagles may be 13 inches tall at the
shoulder and fox hounds approximately double that size, all are
similar in coat, color, ear, tail, and many other characteristics so that one looks like a smaller version of the other.
Similarly, the Welsh terrier looks like a small Airedale, the

Shetland sheep dog like a small collie, the pulik like a small
briard, etc. There are also numerous variations on the spaniel
and setter themes, and there are aspects in which the Saint
Bernard, the mastiff, the Newfoundland, and the Great Pyrenees
resemble one another. Behavioral themes are similarly found
across breeds. Herding dogs, for example, may show great variations among breeds in size and body type, while showing striking similarities in behavior. Paradoxically, the vast differences in form and behavior shown by dogs are only superficial variations in basic canine organization but because they affect
almost every characteristic and can be assembled in various combinations, there is a great deal of variability in almost every
aspect of physical characteristics, temperament and behavior in
which a practical dog breeder might be interested.

In something over 14,000 years of domestication, man discovered and preserved the variations that came to hand and
thereby created the diversity we see in our breeds today. It
is only during the past 75 years that he has been able to use
the tools of modern genetic knowledge to improve his productions
or to understand and analyze what he has done.

Using the Genetic Erector Set

The Stockard experiments and the history of some recently
established breeds illustrate a number of important genetic
principles. One of the most important is that heredity comes
in bits and pieces, and that it is possible by judicious crossing and selection to recombine characteristics among existing
breeds in new patterns. This applies, also, to behavioral
traits. In breeds such as the border collie, where behavior is
paramount, continued selection for the desired behavioral
characteristics has been effective.

A second principle is that selection must be maintained
even after the desired result is obtained. When selection for
behavior is relaxed, it has been the common experience of breeders that the behaviors typical of any given breed may no longer
be counted upon. In the history of the Doberman pinscher, for
example, the initial selection was for dogs that were extremely
"sharp" (easily aroused to attack). When this became trouble-

some and affected the popularity of the br⁀⁀ i, selection for a
more tractable temperament was instituted and has, by and large,
been successful. The great surge of popularity of the German
shepherd dog after World War I stimulated indiscriminate breeding without appropriate selection for temperament, and resulted
in many overly shy and overly sharp dogs. Again, appropriate
selection has been extremely effective in tempering these characteristics. Obviously, it is a practical possibility to improve
the appearance and working qualities of a breed by genetic
means.

Systems of Breeding

Much has been written about line breeding and inbreeding.
It is the popular notion that line breeding is desirable while
inbreeding carries unacceptable risks. Line breeding, of
course, involves inbreeding. It is the objective of any line
breeding program to establish uniformity within the line that
is greater than what would generally be encountered within the
breed, so that dogs belonging to a given line may be expected
to turn out in a particular way with greater certainty than if
they were simply representative of their breed or variety. One
way of accomplishing this is to breed related bitches back to
an outstanding sire, to breed their progeny together and also
continue to breed some of the resulting bitches back to the
foundation sire of the line. While an outstanding dam could
also be used, her capacity for producing progeny is obviously
more limited. The objective, therefore, is to produce a close
genetic relationship to an outstanding dog within the line and
thereby to insure that the desired characteristics will be typical of that line.

Whenever relatives are mated, there is a reduction of
genetic variability because there is an increased chance that
they will be receiving the same genetic contributions through
a common ancestry. This is expressed by the coefficient of
inbreeding, which measures the theoretical increase in genetic
uniformity resulting from the mating of relatives, over the
baseline from which the inbreeding was begun, and can vary from
0-100%. Inbreeding by itself does not imply any selection.

Because of the fact that many genes are recessive and may, there-fore, not be expressed in the presence of a dominant counter-part, and because others are epistatic, which means that their effects are also masked in the presence of other genes, these latent characteristics will be expressed when any form of in-breeding is practiced. When selection will have been for alter-natives to the characteristics that result when these genes come to expression, they will be considered as faults. In some in-stances, they may even be abnormal in the sense that they pro-duce physical anomalies, reduced fertility, reduction in litter size, reduction in individual size, or a general reduction in vigor. In border collies, for example, it has been reported that line breeding has been successful until coefficients of inbreeding of approximately 25 percent are reached, and that at this level of inbreeding, serious problems result (Kelley, 1949). On the other hand, much higher coefficients of inbreeding have been obtained in the Jackson Laboratory program and at Guide Dogs, and these inbred animals are vigorous and conform to type. It follows that inbreeding by itself is neither good nor bad. It involves certain risks and it affords some advantages. The risks are that deleterious combinations of genes will come to expression. The advantages are that where desirable character-istics are displayed, these will breed true within the partially inbred line. Inbreeding with selection will reduce genetic variability, will bring undesirable traits to expression, but at the same time, will also accomplish the development of lines that can be counted upon to breed true to their own character-istics much more predictably than could otherwise obtain. The wastage that occurs is therefore compensated by the greater uniformity of the product.

It should be borne in mind that phenotypic selection that avoids inbreeding maintains a much greater degree of genetic variability and, therefore, a potential for future selection that is lost when inbreeding occurs. The inbreeding coefficient, which expresses the increase in genetic uniformity over the starting point, may also be read as expressing the loss in gene-tic variability, and, therefore, inflexibility for future selec-tion.

The Guide Dog Breeding Program

At Guide Dogs for the Blind, line breeding was practiced for the German shepherd dogs with considerable success. Had only one line been established, the risk that it might at some point fail would have been a serious counterbalance to its advantages. Therefore, three lines were established so that if one of these should run into trouble, it would not be highly probable that similar problems would be encountered in the others at the same time. Even if they were, crosses between the lines would quickly re-establish genetic variability from which to re-select. Within these lines, coefficients of inbreeding approximating 50 percent were achieved with some reduction in litter size, but with no loss of vigor or other adverse effects on the physical and temperamental characteristics of the line-bred dog. This, however, does not necessarily mean that the dogs would be expected to breed true for approximately 50 percent of their genetic characteristics in addition to those that may have already been fixed for the breed when the line breeding program was started. Also, a 50 percent inbreeding coefficient still leaves room for a tremendous amount of genetic and phenotypic variability. Even if there were only 10 variable genes remaining (and the true figure is probably in the hundreds or thousands), and assuming only two expressed phenotypes per gene pair, there would still be 1,024 possible kinds of individuals within the strain. What we do not know, of course, is which genes have been fixed, and, therefore, which phenotypic characteristics will remain relatively constant. Further, since the expression of a given gene is affected by its interaction with other genes, as well as by interactions with environmental events, the most closely inbred dogs may be expected to be far from uniform in the characteristics which they express. However, by comparison with the breed in general, they will show much less variability and the potential for genetic selection from such an inbred base will be reduced in proportion to the reduction of genetic variability.

The Basic Seven -- Guide Dog Foundation Shepherds

As is the case with many successful programs, hindsight is better than foresight. In retrospect, it would have been difficult to decide in advance which dogs to use as the foundation stock for an intense line breeding program. In tracing the actual pedigrees, no great technical genetic knowledge was required in order to institute effective practices. The dogs originally acquired for the program were good representatives of their breed with respect to conformation and working qualities. In spite of this, the initial success was small. Some of this may be attributable to less than optimal conditions of rearing and to uninformed methods of selecting dogs for training. (The former has been thoroughly discussed elsewhere in this book.) However, there was an obvious genetic component. During the ten-year period from 1942-1952, over 700 German shepherd puppies were produced in matings involving 62 bitches and 50 males. When a successful mating occurred, as judged by the success of the progeny in becoming guide dogs, it was very often repeated. If the repeated matings were also successful, this stock was saved for breeding and particularly for line breeding with a successful sire. His daughters and granddaughters, as well as collateral bitches, were bred back to him, and some of these descendants were also mated with each other. It was found that the greatest success was obtained when the degree of genetic relationship to an outstanding sire or dam became greater than that obtained in a son or daughter. Close line breeding with its attendant inbreeding was, therefore, practiced with excellent success. When the selection program was evaluated, it was found that every German shepherd dog that was successful in the breeding program, on the basis of a high proportion of its progeny becoming successful guide dogs, traced back to only seven animals -- five bitches and two males (Fig. 8.2). There were surprisingly few problems encountered in the inbreeding, if care was exercised in selecting parents that did not show similar faults and that exhibited physical vigor and behavioral stability. One unexpected factor that emerged from these studies was that the age of the mother in repeat matings influenced the success of the progeny (See Table 9.6). Bitches

Figure 8.2. Foundation stock. Shown are 4 of the Basic Seven German shepherds. ABOVE, left, Frank of Ledge Acres; right, Guide Dog's Doris. BELOW, left, Orkos of Longworth; right, Katrina von Siegfriedheim with puppies. (Photos by Virginia Beauchamp.)

Honor

Figure 8.3. Honor, a typical German shepherd bitch resulting from selective breeding.

beyond their fifth or sixth year produced litters that were less successful than when they were younger, although occasional litters from older bitches were highly successful in several instances where these older bitches had previously had truly outstanding success records.

Genetic Restructuring

In examining these aspects of the work, it is important to note that the selection did not merely preserve the characteristics of the original foundation stock, but improved upon them in ways that were important for the particular mission that the dogs had to serve. The German shepherd dog had not previously been selected to move at the pace of a human being. This is a powerful breed with a loping gait that can cover great distances at a relatively rapid pace. In selecting them for the specialized requirements of leading the blind, it was found that many

of them pulled too hard, had a gait that would wobble the
harness, and were generally not physically adapted to the life
of a human city dweller. A somewhat smaller, cobbier dog appeared to do better under these conditions (Fig. 8.3).

In addition, the protective temperament useful in guard
dogs could prevent a dog from transfering its attachments, first
from the person who had raised it to the trainer, and later to
the blind person for whom it would have to take responsibility.
Where these transfers were successfully accomplished, it was
highly desirable that this responsibility should not take the
form of being overly protective when in harness. In sum, it
was necessary to select for a somewhat different physical and
temperamental type than was represented in the initial stock,
and this was achieved by selection and inbreeding from among
the progeny of only two sires and five dams. No outside stock
having a different conformation, gait, or temperament was introduced after the early stages of the program.

In terms of what has already been described, we know that
a great deal of genetic variability for every aspect of the
structure and behavior of the dog exists within a given breed.
The selection practiced by breeders for the working qualities
and conformation of the breed does not seriously restrict this
variability. There are numerous genetic combinations that are
compatible with a limited range of physical and behavioral norms
as defined by a breed standard. Had these basic seven dogs be-
longed to a closely inbred strain to begin with, this variability would have been seriously restricted to the point where it
would not have been possible to change the characteristics of
their progeny by selection. On the contrary, inspection of
their pedigrees reveals that there was virtually no inbreeding
as measured by the occurrence of the same individual more than
once in a six generation pedigree. As long as this amount of
genetic variability exists, it is possible, as demonstrated in
the guide dog program, to re-structure the phenotype by reshuf-
fling existing genes without going outside of the parental
stock.

It should also be noted that what constitutes an "improvement" for one purpose is not necessarily an improvement for
another. A guard dog and a guide dog need different qualifica-

tions. The German shepherd dog with its history of versatility contains within its genetic make-up those ingredients that permit the specialization of particular lines for particular purposes. This is what was accomplished in the breeding program for Guide Dogs for the Blind.

Unfortunately, by the time the genetic data were analyzed, it was too late to save the foundation stock. However, the knowledge derived from both the retrospective analysis of the data and the conscious attempt to line breed from the dogs available at the time the research program was active has provided a blueprint for the genetic production and optimal rearing of such stock for any future program.

Evaluating the Adult

Another crucial time to assess the potential performance of a dog is when it is brought in as an adult for training. During the first few days, the dogs are placed in their kennel runs at the school, are examined and evaluated in various ways. The optimal time for evaluating the adult is after he has become accustomed to his new premises and routine and before he has become attached to a particular handler or trainer. For shepherds, the optimal time was usually about four days. For retrievers, it was a few days longer. Our best predictions resulted from quietly approaching the dog in its run and calling it by name in a soft, calm voice. The dog was not previously familiar with the person doing the testing. Testing was done from the inside pen and the door to the outside run was open so that the dog could approach or withdraw over the entire distance of the run.

Goldens and Labradors that did not approach readily when called, or that appeared timid or defensive, generally turned out to be poor risks. This was particularly true where the dog did not approach within approximately a 30 second period. Shepherds, on the other hand, that took as long as a minute and a half to make up their minds were likely to succeed, if the latency period appeared to involve caution rather than fear (tail tucked, slinking gait, trembling, or drooling) or aggressive threats combined with lack of approach. The test, therefore, must be used in different ways to evaluate different

breeds, but in our hands it was 70-80 percent accurate in predicting problem dogs. The key factors in the success of the
test are that the tester should be a stranger, that the test
should be performed before the dog has become accustomed to
being handled by a particular person at the school, and at the
point when it has become somewhat territorial about its run.

Hip Dysplasia

An important physical fault found in many breeds is that
of hip dysplasia*. Breeders have long been alert to the problem
and many have invested tremendous efforts in attempting to breed
it out of their stocks. It is common practice to X-ray sires
and dams and to breed only from those that show no signs of hip
dysplasia, and to guarantee that puppies will be free of it, or
that they will be replaced.

Here, as in other areas where heredity and environment are
presumed to interact, there has been much heat and confusion
with respect to the overall management of this condition within
a breed. One source of confusion is what the implication of
varying degrees of subluxation might be for the working ability
of the dog. Among guide dogs in service, a number of those dis-
playing moderate degrees of subluxation have shown no sign of
lameness, and have not had their working life shortened or
otherwise made less useful because of this condition (See Table
6.9). Although there may be some relationship between malforma-
tions of the hip joints and other secondary complications, such
as arthritis and calcifications, both of which may be painful
and may interfere with the dog's ability to work, these condi-

*A representative literature on hip dysplasia follows: Born-
fors et al., 1964; Carnahan et al., 1968; Forsyth and Paschall,
1963; Gibson, 1967; Gofton, 1971; Harris, 1960; Harris et al.,
1962; Henricson and Olsson, 1959; Hutt, 1967, 1969; Johnston
and Cox, 1970; Jones, 1969; Kaman and Gossling, 1967; Kelley et
al., 1959; Larsen and Corley, 1971; Lawson, 1968; Lust and Baker,
1970; McClave, 1957; Pierce and Bridges, 1967; Riser, 1963a, b,
c, 1967, 1969; Riser et al., 1964; Riser and Shirer, 1964;
Robinson, 1968; Salter, 1968; Schales, 1956, 1957; Schnelle,
1954, 1959; Seer and Hurov, 1969; Snavely, 1959; Sprinkle and
Krook, 1970; Townsend et al., 1971; Trueta and Morgan, 1960;
Whittington et al., 1961; Woolf, 1971; Woolf et al., 1968.

tions can also occur in animals that have perfectly normal hips.

It used to be thought that the weight of the dog was a factor, and, therefore, that puppies should not be overfed at the time when their bones were developing. This explanation became less tenable when hip dysplasia began to be encountered in very small breeds. The role of the hip musculature was also the subject of discussion and evaluation, since it was at first believed that coursing dogs, such as Greyhounds, that had been selected for well developed musculature and skeletal soundness, were free of hip dysplasia. Subsequently, it was encountered in these breeds as well.

The problem when one is concerned about a particular dog or group of dogs that are to be used for working purposes is how to maximize the potential of the stock in hand. The contributions of diet and exercise therefore receive a good deal of attention, since both of these factors are manipulable. The idea of breeding from only "perfect" dogs is also a practical one, and the hope within a controlled breeding program is that one would be able to eliminate the genetic predisposition for hip dysplasia from the stock entirely.

In collaboration with the late Theodore Hage, D.V.M., of the University of California at Davis, we initiated a thorough study of hip dysplasia and arranged the resulting X-rays according to pedigree, in order that the genetic factors could be evaluated. Inspection of these data showed that hip dysplasia was not a single entity, as had been thought by some students of this condition. They had the plausible theory that the hip socket and joint must develop in relation to each other and that there is some sort of feedback mechanism between the two. The Hage evidence was more in line with the Stockard results on morphological variation -- namely, that each structure could vary independently genetically. Thus, the acetabulum could be well rounded and provide a good socket into which the head of the femur could fit, or it could vary all the way from slight imperfections to a flattened and inadequate socket. Similarly, the head of the femur, which fits into the hip socket, could be well rounded, slightly flattened or otherwise reduced or distorted. Each could vary independently of the other. An additional source of variation came from the angle that the head of

178

Figure 8.4. Hip dysplasia. Schematic drawings illustrating
the various possible defects of the left hip joint. Numbers
correspond to the descriptions in the score sheet illustrated
in Figure 8.5. In practice, X-ray photographs were taken of
both hips, tracings were made, and each hip scored according
to the degree and number of defects as indicated on the scale.
A dog with perfect hips received 30 points for each hip, for
a total possible score of 60. (Continued on opposite page.)

ACETABULUM

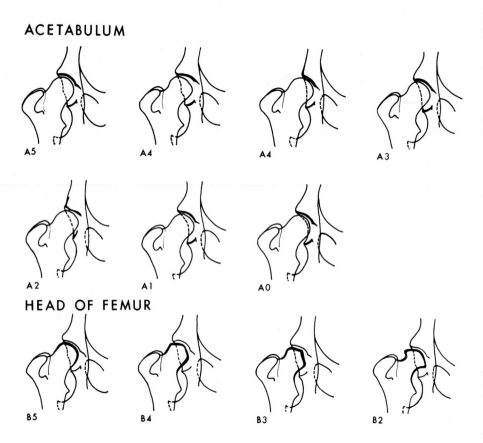

HEAD OF FEMUR

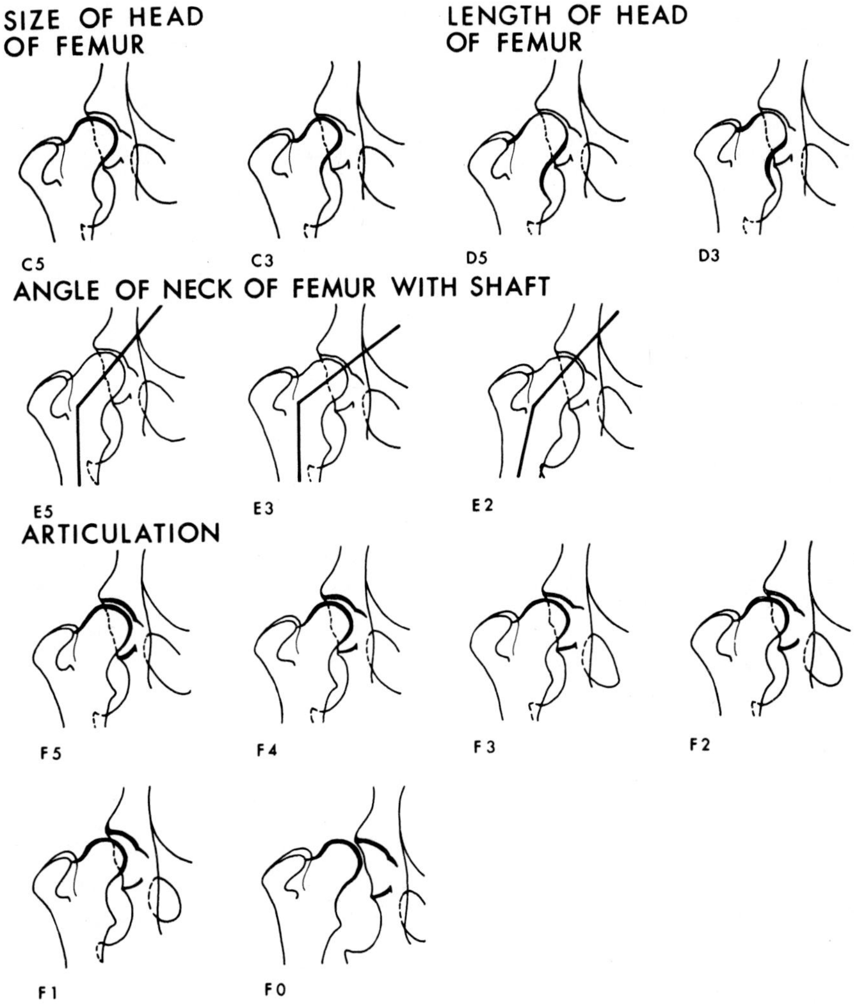

SIZE OF HEAD OF FEMUR

LENGTH OF HEAD OF FEMUR

C5 C3 D5 D3

ANGLE OF NECK OF FEMUR WITH SHAFT

E5 E3 E2

ARTICULATION

F5 F4 F3 F2

F1 F0

the femur makes with the shaft. The normal angle permits the leg to swing freely in the proper plane underneath the body. If the angle becomes too large, and if the head of the femur is firmly seated in the acetabulum, the leg tends to straddle out to the side.

On the basis of our information, the conformation of the hip depends upon a number of independently inherited variations that can occur in any combination with respect to each other. Where the socket is simply somewhat shallow, or the head of the femur is small, or flattened, or both, a compensatory development of the hip musculature could serve to keep the joint in functional order. Where, however, the angle between the head and neck of the femur and the shaft is too straight, the leg would be in an abnormal position if the head of the femur were pulled securely into the socket.

Using one of the conventional 5-point scales on which to rate the dogs, we found that this was insufficient for genetic selection. Some dogs rated as completely normal by this method when mated to others with presumably "perfect" hips produced puppies with varying degrees of hip dysplasia. The distribution of puppies from dogs exhibiting moderate degrees of hip dysplasia included the entire range of variation from very poor to very excellent hips.

Several conclusions can be drawn from these results: one is that the various parts of the hip structure are independently inherited. Another is that dogs rated as completely normal on a 5-point scale can transmit genetic factors for hip dysplasia. The fact that dogs that show some deviations from normality can reconstitute the entire range of variation when bred together indicates that there are a number of independently inherited genetic factors involved, and that genetic variation for a number of these is occurring such that when the genetic cards are shuffled, all possible combinations can, in theory, be realized, and, in practice, many of them are. Dogs having very poor hips will, for the most part, produce puppies with poor hips. Dogs in the middle of the range may produce puppies like themselves, or worse, or much better. Dogs having very good hips may produce progeny like themselves, but in a significant number of cases, the progeny will show varying degrees

Case No. _____ Sire _____ Sex _____ Date of Whelp _____

Breed _____ Dam _____ Dog No. _____ Age in Months _____

		Right		Left	
RADIOLOGICAL ANALYSIS - ADULT HIP DYSPLASIA		Rating	Card Col.	Rating	Card Col.
A Acetabulum	Well rounded with complete anterior brim	5		5	
	Anterior brim incomplete or straight	4		4	
	Slightly shallow	3		3	
	Local, non-arthritic malformations	2		2	
	Shallow	1		1	
	Very Shallow	0		0	
B Head of Femur	Well rounded	5		5	
	Slightly flattened	4		4	
	Slightly flattened	3		3	
	Flattened	3		3	
	Flattened and distorted	2		2	
C Size of Head of Femur	Normal	5		5	
	Small	3		3	
D Length of Neck of Femur	Normal	5		5	
	Short	3		3	
E Angle of Neck of Femur with Shaft	$135° - 140°$	5		5	
	Coxa vara - less than $135°$	3		3	
	Coxa valga - more than $140°$	2		2	
F Articulation	Well seated with even articular space	5		5	
	Well seated, but articular space not even	4		4	
	Fairly well seated, articular space not even	3		3	
	Poorly seated	2		2	
	Subluxation	1		1	
	Complete luxation	0		0	
Scores (sums of ratings for each hip)					
Total Score (sum of ratings for both hips)		Card Col.		Rating	

Figure 8.5. Data sheet for radiological analysis involving both hips. A dog with perfect hips receives a score of 60.

of hip dysplasia.

Starting with the last findings, the X-rays of those sires and dams who had entirely normal hips by conventional criteria were analyzed using matings where they were bred to each other. We then separated those matings that bred true for hip conformation from those that did not. Careful tracings were made of the upper portion of the femur, including the head, neck and shaft, and of the acetabulum (Figs. 8.4, 8.5). It was found that among those rated as "normal" some were more normal than others, in that slight imperfections could be found in the roundness of the socket, the size or roundness of the femur, or variations in the angle between the shaft of the femur and the head and neck. Using tracings made from the X-rays and the pedigrees of more than 200 dogs, it was possible, using the Hage scales, to detect variations having scores of 30 to 7 -- from the most ideal configurations through the range of deviations exhibited in the pedigrees. In some cases, these were more pronounced in one hip than in the other. We therefore used a 60-point rating scale (30 for each hip) in classifying the X-rays. It is important to note that the position in which the dog is X-rayed is critical in order to be certain that all deviations are detected. Sometimes repeat X-rays were required, and, in all, up to four X-rays per dog were used.

Using the 60-point rating scale, it became clear that a number of dogs that appeared to show no hip dysplasia based on a 5-point scale showed detectable minor anomalies when their X-rays were compared to tracings made from the most ideal hips in the colony. Breeding from such specimens did upgrade the population, but those that were perfect on a 5-point scale and were not so on the 60-point scale did produce puppies with varying degrees of hip dysplasia, although, in general, their progeny were much better in this respect than were those of dogs that did not rate as high. Our data suggest that carriers of imperfections can be detected and that selection based on finer discriminations, as represented by our 60-point scale, would go a long way towards ameliorating the problem. It has also been our observation that animals showing various degrees and kinds of hip dysplasia also show anomalies with respect to shoulder placement and the alignment of the front legs.

The Whole Dog

So far as genetic selection is concerned, the challenge to the breeder is that the hereditary factors are parceled out and recombined. Selection for perfect hips, if completely successful, would not accomplish much if, at the same time, other qualities were allowed to deteriorate. The guide dog must be highly intelligent, willing, stable, physically sound, responsible, not overly protective, and well balanced. There is a good deal of genetic variability underlying all of these attributes, and to fix any combination of them at an ideal and uniform level would be difficult, if not impossible. While large breeding programs, such as the one at Guide Dogs for the Blind, are invaluable for providing the data needed for an understanding that will permit better breeding practices, there will continue to be genetic variability, even with close line breeding. One must not permit selection for one or two attributes to outweigh the balance that is required to produce an all around sound specimen.

The experience from the Guide Dogs program shows that it is possible by a combination of rearing, testing, and selective breeding practices to vastly improve the working potential of a given breed or stock in a relatively short time. Since the stock will not be uniform, it will have the potential for deteriorating, as well as for getting better. It would, therefore, be prudent to select for several lines in the event that one or another runs into trouble; this will also provide a potential for creating a pool of greater genetic variability by intercrossing among the lines and reselecting.

REFERENCES

Bornfors, S., Palsson, K., and Skude, G. Hereditary aspects of hip dysplasia in German shepherd dogs. J. Amer. Vet. Med. Assoc., 1964, 145, 15.

Burns, M. and Fraser, M. N. Genetics of the Dog. Philadelphia: J. B. Lippincott, 1966.

Carnahan, D. L., Guffy, M. M., Hibbs, C. M., Leipold, H. W. and
Huston, K. Hip Dysplasia in Hereford cattle. J. Amer.
Vet. Med. Assoc., 1968, 152, 1151-1157.

Forsyth, H. F. and Paschall, H. A. Genetics of congenital hip
dysplasia. J. Bone & Joint Surg., 1963, 45-A, 1781.

Gibson, D. A. Congenital dislocation of the hip: a review of
adults treated in childhood. Canad. J. Surg., 1967, 10,
288-298.

Ginsburg, B. E. Breeding structure and social behavior of
mammals: a servo-mechanism for the avoidance of panmixia.
In: D. Glass (Ed.), Genetics, Biology and Behavior. New
York: Rockefeller University Press and Russell Sage Foundation, 1968, pp. 117-128.

Ginsburg, B. E. Anxiety: a behavioural legacy. In: Physiol-
ogy, Emotion and Psychosomatic Illness. Ciba Foundation
Symposium 8. Amsterdam: Elsevier, 1972, pp. 163-174.

Ginsburg, B. E. Evolution of communication patterns in animals.
In: E. C. Simmel and M. E. Hahn (Eds.), Communicative
Behavior and Evolution. New York: Academic Press, 1976,
pp. 59-79.

Gofton, J. P. Studies in osteoarthritis of the hip: Part III.
Congenital subluxation and osteoarthritis of the hip.
Canad. Med. Assoc. J., 1971, 104, 911-915.

Harris, W. H. A microscopic method of determining rates of
bone growth. Nature, 1960, 188, 1038-1039.

Harris, W. H., Jackson, R. H. and Jowsey, J. The in vivo distribution of tetracyclines in canine bone. J. Bone &
Joint Surg., 1962, 44-A, 1038.

Henricson, B. and Olsson, S. E. Hereditary acetabular dysplasia
in German shepherd dogs. J. Amer. Vet. Med. Assoc., 1959,
135, 207.

Hutt, F. B. Genetic selection to reduce the incidence of hip
dysplasia in dogs. J. Amer. Vet. Med. Assoc., 1967, 151,
1041-1048.

Hutt, F. B. Advances in canine genetics, with special reference
to hip dysplasia. Canad. Vet. J., 1969, 10, 307-311.

Johnston, D. E. and Cox, B. The incidence in purebred dogs in
Australia of abnormalities that may be inherited. Aust.
Vet. J., 1970, 46, 465-474.

Jones, B. S. Upper femoral osteotomy in the treatment of para-
lytic subluxation of the hip due to poliomyelitis. S.
Afr. Med. J., 1969, 43, 1187-1192.

Kaman, C. H. and Gossling, H. R. A breeding program to reduce
hip dysplasia in German shepherd dogs. J. Amer. Vet. Med.
Assoc., 1967, 151, 562-571.

Kelley, R. B. Sheep Dogs. Sydney, Australia: Halstead Press,
1949.

Kelley, P. J., Janes, J. M., and Patterson, P. A. The effect
of arteriovenous fistulae on the vascular pattern of the
femora of immature dogs, a microangiographic study. J.
Bone & Joint Surg., 1959, 41A, 1101.

Larsen, S. and Corley, E. A. Radiographic evaluations in a
canine hip dysplasia control program. J. Amer. Vet. Med.
Assoc., 1971, 159, 989-992.

Lawson, D. D. Hip dysplasia in the dog. Vet. Rec., 1968, 83,
655-656.

Little, C. C. Inheritance of Coat Color in Dogs. Ithaca:
Cornell University Press, 1957.

Lust, G. and Baker, J. A. Altered protein metabolism in muscle
and cartilage associated with congenital malformation of
hip joints in dogs. Fed. Proc., 1970, 29, 551.

McClave, P. L. Elimination of coxofemoral dysplasia from a
breeding kennel. Vet. Med., 1957, 52, 241.

Pfaffenberger, C. The New Knowledge of Dog Behavior. New York:
Howell Book House, 1963.

Pierce, K. R. and Bridges, C. H. The role of estrogens in the
pathogenesis of canine hip dysplasia. Metabolism of exo-
genous estrogens. J. Small Anim. Pract., 1967, 8, 383-389.

Riser, W. H. An analysis of the current status of hip dysplasia
in the dog. J. Amer. Vet. Med. Assoc., 1963a, 144, 709.

Riser, W. H. A new look at developmental subluxation and dislocation, hip dysplasia in the dog. J. Small Anim. Pract.,
1963b, 4, 421.

Riser, W. H. Hip dysplasia in dogs. Proc. 17th World Vet.
Congr., 1963c, 2, 1099.

Riser, W. H. Correlation between canine hip dysplasia and pel-
vic muscle mass: a study of 95 dogs. Amer. J. Vet. Res.,
1967, 28, 769-777.

Riser, W. H. Progress in canine hip dysplasia control. J. Amer. Vet. Med. Assoc., 1969, 155, 2047-2052.

Riser, W. H. and Shirer, J. F. A new look at canine hip dysplasia. Amer. Vet. Med. Assoc. Proc., 1964, 101, 142.

Riser, W. H., et al. Influence of early rapid growth and weight gain on hip dysplasia in the German shepherd dog. J. Amer. Vet. Med. Assoc., 1964, 145, 661.

Robinson, G. W. Birth characteristics of children with congenital dislocation of the hip. Amer. J. Epidemiol., 1968, 87, 275-284.

Salter, R. B. Etiology, pathogenesis and possible prevention of congenital dislocation of the hip. Canad. Med. Assoc. J., 1968, 98, 933-945.

Schales, O. Genetic aspects of dysplasia of the hip joints. N. Amer. Vet., 1956, 37, 476.

Schales, O. Hereditary patterns in dysplasia of the hips. N. Amer. Vet., 1957, 38, 152.

Schnelle, G. B. Congenital dysplasia of the hip (canine) and sequellae. Proceedings Book of the American Veterinary Medical Association, 1954, 253.

Schnelle, G. B. Canine hip dysplasia. Lab. Investigation, 1959, 8, 1178.

Scott, J. P. and Fuller, J. L. Genetics and the Social Behavior of the Dog. Chicago: University of Chicago Press, 1965.

Seer, G. and Hurov, L. Elbow dysplasia in dogs with hip dysplasia. J. Amer. Vet. Med. Assoc., 1969, 154, 631-637.

Snavely, J. G. The genetic aspects of hip dysplasia in dogs. J. Amer. Vet. Med. Assoc., 1959, 135, 201.

Sprinkle, T. A. and Krook, L. Hip dysplasia, elbow dysplasia, and "eosinophilic panosteitis." Three clinical manifestations of hyperestrinism in the dog? Cornel. Vet., 1970, 60, 476-490.

Stockard, C. R., Anderson, O. D. and James, W. T. The Genetic and Endocrine Basis for Differences in Form and Behavior. Philadelphia: The Wistar Institute of Anatomy and Biology, 1941.

Townsend, L. R., Gillette, E. L. and Lebel, J. L. Progression of hip dysplasia in military working dogs. J. Amer. Vet. Med. Assoc., 1971, 159, 1129-1133.

Trueta, J. and Morgan. The vascular contribution to osteogenesis – injection studies. J. Bone & Joint Surg., 1960, 42B, 97-109.

Whittington, K., Banks, W. C., Carlson, W. D., Hoerlein, B. F., Husted, P. W., Leonard, E. F., McClave, P. L., Rhodes, W. H., Riser, W. H. and Schnelle, G. B. Report of the A.V.M.A. Panel on Canine Hip Dysplasia. J. Amer. Vet. Med. Assoc., 1961, 139, 791-806.

Winge, O. Inheritance in Dogs with Special Reference to Hunting Breeds. (Translated by C. Roberts). New York: Comstock Publishing Company, 1950.

Woolf, C. M. Congenital hip disease: Implications of genetic counseling. Soc. Biol., 1971, 18, 10-17.

Woolf, C. M., Koehn, J. H. and Coleman, S. S. Congenital hip disease in Utah: The influence of genetic and nongenetic factors. Amer. J. Hum. Genet., 1968, 20, 430-439.

THE LOGISTICS OF GUIDE DOG PRODUCTION

John L. Fuller

The word _logistics_ was originally applied to the planning
and organization of military supply systems. As applied to the
making of a guide dog, it refers to the design of a breeding,
rearing, and training program which will make a quota of dogs
available for a class of blind persons at some time in the future. We have already described the general training and rearing procedures as they were carried out at Guide Dogs for the
Blind, Inc. In this chapter we shall be concerned with the
quantitative aspects of producing guide dogs, the factors af-
fecting fertility of dams, survival of offspring, and rejections
from the program for physical or behavioral inadequacy. By
discussing some of these factors from a historical point of
view, we can visualize more clearly some of the changes that
have improved the program.

Efficiency can be measured by the cost per unit produced,
but for our purposes it has been more useful to measure it by
the _utilization rate_, which we can define as the proportion of
dogs raised which become guides. For various purposes we have
taken different bases, sometimes the total number of puppies
born, sometimes the number surviving to eight weeks of age,
sometimes the number entering training. The reasons for the
changing base will be clear as we proceed. Often it is convenient in discussing losses to define an index of attrition as
the proportion of puppies lost to the program during a particular phase. In general we have calculated rate of utilization
and indices of attrition for groups composed of all puppies
born in one calendar year. Thus, the whelp of 1960 contains
all dogs born from January 1 through December 31 of that year.

The utilization and attrition indices have the virtue of
being quantitative, thus permitting comparisons between differ-

ent breeds of dogs, different methods of management, and different years. Such comparisons must be made with care, however. The utilization index is subject to the law of supply and demand. When the supply of puppies is high with respect to the need for guides, fewer of the available animals will be graduated because there is no room for them. Under such conditions the rate of utilization would fall, but this should not be interpreted as a decrease in the quality of the animals produced. Good management dictates that there should be a modest amount of overproduction of puppies in order to be prepared for emergencies.

The gross attrition index calculated on the total loss of puppies from birth to failure in the final training program is not particularly useful as a guide to management. The reasons for loss at different stages of the program must be classified in order to see where the major problems lie. This procedure was carried out for 1136 puppies of 3 breeds, the entire output of the Guide Dogs for the Blind breeding program between 1958 and 1962, a period during which basic rearing and training procedures were relatively constant. Table 9.1 summarizes the losses during five phases of guide dog production, and shows the number which survived all hazards to become guides or to be added to the breeding stock.

During this period a little more than one-fourth of the puppies born alive became guides and eight percent were added to breeding stock. Thus one-third of the animals born were of economic value to the institution and the people it serves. There were two great sources of loss: slightly more than one-fourth were puppies dying in infancy and slightly less than one-fourth were rejected during training. Losses in training are much more serious economically, for the investment in the animal at this time includes kennel costs, puppy testing, rearing in the 4-H home, and the effort of the trainers. Nevertheless, the cost of puppy deaths is not inconsiderable. A reduction by one-half in the puppy death rate would permit a decrease of about 13 percent in the number of dogs kept as breeding stock, as fewer bitches would be required to produce the needed number of puppies.

Table 9.2 summarizes the same data in a somewhat different

Table 9.1

ATTRITION AT SEPARABLE PHASES OF GUIDE DOG PRODUCTION
(All Puppies Whelped 1958-1962)

	German Shepherd	Golden Retriever	Labrador Retriever	Sum	Percent
Born	735	241	117	1093	100.0
Fees*	2	8	0	11	1.0
Died (0-8 weeks)	243	30	38	311	27.6
Lost from program (8-13 weeks)	46	16	2	64	5.5
(4-H Home)	50	13	7	70	6.1
Before Training	18	2	0	20	1.7
In Training	148	59	26	233	24.1
Retained for Breeding	64	13	13	90	8.0
Issued as Guides	163	100	31	294	26.1

*Puppies supplied to others to compensate for stud service or loan of a brood bitch.

format. The most striking feature of this table is the preponderance of behavioral causes of rejection over physical causes in puppies over 8 weeks of age. These two tables explain the focus of the entire research program. Effort was directed primarily upon those phases of the operation in which the greatest benefits might be forthcoming. Behavioral faults might conceivably be reduced by genetic selection for temperament and learning ability, or by better specification of rearing and training procedures. Even if these techniques were not completely successful, there would be value in discovering potential misfits early. Early deaths might be reduced by selection against deleterious genes, by selection for good maternal care and by improved management practices in the whelping kennel. Deaths after 8 weeks of age and rejections for physical reasons each amounted to about 10 percent attrition. Although they offer

Table 9.2

RELATIVE FREQUENCY OF CAUSES OF ATTRITION IN THE
THREE MOST WIDELY USED BREEDS

(Puppies Whelped 1958-1962)

Cause of Loss	German Shepherds		Golden Retrievers		Labrador Retrievers		Combined	
	No.	%	No.	%	No.	%	No.	%
Death (0-8 weeks)	243	46.1	30	23.1	38	46.9	311	42.2
Death (over 8 wks.)	59	11.2	9	6.9	5	6.2	73	9.9
Physical fault	48	9.1	17	13.1	10	12.3	75	10.1
Behavioral fault	177	33.6	74	56.9	28	34.6	279	37.8
Total Losses	527		130		81		738	

opportunity for constructive recommendations, the economic benefits from improvement will be less important. These considerations explain the emphasis of this report.

These tables are incomplete in a sense for they cover only
the time preceding actual service to a blind person. Here,
indeed, is the payoff of the entire effort. We have chosen to
present the material on this part of the guide dog's life history in a separate chapter, for it occurred in a context in
which the institution had less control than at earlier periods,
and under conditions which were not as open for study by our
research staff.

Because comparative data were unavailable, it is difficult
to estimate the degree to which losses could have been reduced.
It is unrealistic to expect every puppy to become a guide or a
member of the breeding stock. As shown below, the achieved
utilization rate of 33% represented a substantial improvement
over experience at Guide Dogs for the Blind in its early years.
If one based the utilization rate on puppies living to 8 weeks
of age, the value rose to about 50%. We suspect that 50% of
puppies born is an attainable rate of utilization, but reaching
this goal would require extraordinary effort and careful planning.

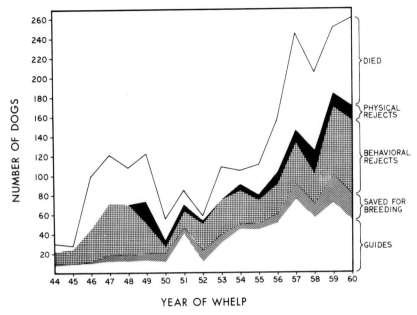

Figure 9.1.   Annual fluctuations in the production and utilization of puppies.

Annual Fluctuations in Attrition Rate

The production records for eighteen years classified according to the scheme of Table 9.2 are shown in Figure 9.1.
The growth of services provided by Guide Dogs for the Blind is
shown both in the numbers of puppies born and in the numbers of
guide dogs trained.   Fluctuations in the amount of attrition
attributable to broad classes of factors are clearly shown, but
must be regarded with some caution.   The apparently lower mortality prior to 1956, for example, was undoubtedly due to the
fact that records of the numbers of puppies whelped were not
kept prior to that year.   Puppies appeared in the registry at
about 6 to 8 weeks of age when they entered the testing program.
Rejections for physical reasons were not recorded before 1949
when they appear at a value higher than in any subsequent year.
Behavioral rejection was consistently high except for 1950, but
the more detailed records showed variation in the time of such
rejection.   From 1951 on puppies were disqualified more frequently on the basis of their puppy tests.

These data included all breeds in varying proportions and
covered a period in which there were changes in procedure and
in personnel. We believe that it would be difficult to analyze
the complete data so as to identify the factors that produced
large swings in the proportion of successfully trained guides
from year to year. Thus a more detailed study was made of the
puppies whelped from 1958 to 1962, and the findings are reported
below.

Attrition from Early Deaths

A loss of 27.6% between birth and 8 weeks of age may seem
exceptionally high. Estimates from other colonies of purebred
dogs range from 10 to 30 percent (Corbin, et.al., 1962). The
Guide Dogs for the Blind colony fell within this range, but
clearly at the upper end. Most of the colonies reviewed by
Corbin et. al. were used in nutrition research, and the bitches
may have been better nourished than animals kept in private
homes. Some bitches might have been emotionally upset by the
transfer from their boarding home to the Guide Dogs for the
Blind kennels, and so gave poorer care to their puppies than
they would if such transfers were unnecessary. A comparison
may be made with the purebred colony of Scott and Fuller (1965)
in which neonatal mortality (here defined as prior to 3 weeks)
was 14.4% of 327 births, and mortality to one year was 18.3%.
Mortality among hybrids (basenji x cocker spaniel) was less
than one-half these values. Clearly the selection and inbreeding practiced with pure breeds has resulted in the retention
and dissemination of deleterious recessive genes whose effects
are manifested in early deaths. There is no evidence that selection and inbreeding as practiced at Guide Dogs for the Blind
has worsened the infant mortality, but it seems possible that
selection for high survival (good maternal care) might reduce
early deaths by as much as one-half, bringing them into the
range reported by Scott and Fuller.

A striking feature of the data is the tendency for litters
to either survive as a whole or to show relatively severe losses of varying degrees. This is demonstrated by Table 9.3
which shows the survival rate up to 8 weeks of 114 matings,

Table 9.3

DISTRIBUTION OF SURVIVAL RATES (8 WEEKS OF AGE)
AMONG 114 MATINGS (MOSTLY ONE LITTER EACH)

Percent of Survival	Number of Matings
0-10	6
11-20	2
21-30	3
31-40	2
41-50	5
51-60	8
61-70	13
71-80	8
81-90	16
91-100	51

mostly producing one litter each. Only eight matings had survival rates close to the "average" (72%), while 45% of the litters showed 100% survival. Losses thus are not evenly distributed among litters. The pattern suggests causes such as in-
fectious disease spreading by contact among all members of an
afflicted litter, poor intrauterine condition, premature birth,
and neglect on the part of the bitch of her entire brood.

Litter survival among the three major breeds used at Guide
Dogs for the Blind is compared in Table 9.4. Here litters are
classified into only three groups, low, high, and complete.
Shepherds had proportionately more low survival litters, goldens
rated highest in complete survival litters, while Labradors had
losses widely distributed among litters. The differences between breeds are highly significant (Chi square = 15.06; d.f. =
4; p < .01).

No evidence was found for superior litter survival at particular seasons. There was an association between high mortality and a period of shortage of experienced personnel in the

Table 9.4

COMPARISON OF LITTER SURVIVAL AMONG
THREE BREEDS, 1958-1962

| | | Survival Rate | | | Total |
		Under 50%	50-99%	100%	Number
German	Number	22	49	27	98
Shepherd	Percent	22	50	28	
Golden	Number	2	11	16	29
Retriever	Percent	7	38	55	
Labrador	Number	2	14	2	18
Retriever	Percent	11	78	11	
TOTAL	Number	26	74	45	145
	Percent	18	51	31	

kennels, but cause and effect cannot be proven. In any case,
if anything goes wrong with a young litter, it can best be rem-
edied if noticed and corrected immediately.

Attrition During Training

Animals were lost from the program following puppy tests
and during their stay in 4-H homes. These losses were discussed
in other chapters. Because they were not numerous it was difficult to find significant trends with respect to time or important differences among breeds. Attrition during training,
particularly for behavioral reasons, was a more serious problem.

A convenient index of training efficiency is the ratio:

$$\frac{\text{Number of dogs becoming guides.}}{\text{Number of dogs entering training.}}$$

In many ways this index is the best measure of the genetic quality of the stock and the adequacy of home and kennel environment. In the dogs whelped during 1958-1962, the proportion becoming guides was 51.8%. Among the remainder, 41.0% failed for
behavioral reasons, 5.2% were failed for physical reasons (main-
ly cosmetic*) and 1.7% died during training. The ratio of suc-

---

*Cosmetic: yellow teeth, crooked ears or other physical traits
that might cause a blind owner to be ashamed of his dog.

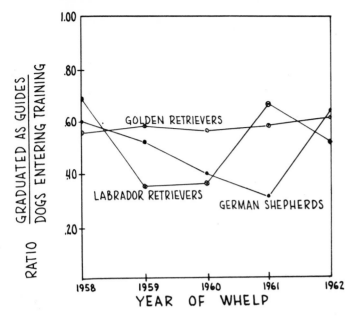

Figure 9.2. Fluctuations in the training efficiency index during a 5-year period. Compare with Figure 3.1.

cess varied among the breeds and also fluctuated widely from year to year (Figure 9.2).

The significant points in this figure are the uniformity of percentage of success in training among the goldens and the fluctuations among shepherds and Labradors. The ratio of success dropped steadily in shepherds from 1958 to 1961 (60% to 32%) and then rose abruptly in the whelp of 1962 (trained in 1963 and 1964). Fluctuations in the Labradors were more irregular, possibly because the number of individuals was much smaller.

The variation in success from year to year was great enough to cause concern, and to make planning difficult. More puppies must be reared if the percentage of failures increases. Several possible causes of the fluctuations, particularly genetic causes, were investigated. The inbreeding coefficients of the shepherds of the 1962 whelp were lower on the average than those of the 1961 whelp. In the 1961 group 40% of animals with inbreeding coefficients between .11 and .20 became guides; in 1962, 77% were successful. For animals with inbreeding coefficients over

.20 the corresponding figures were for 1961, 32%; for 1962, 52%.
Although the less inbred shepherds had a slightly better record,
the more inbred group shared in the upswing of the 1962 whelp.
Inbreeding cannot be the main factor in causing the annual fluctuation.

Changes in success from year to year might be caused by
shifts in the genetic composition of the tested group. One
should expect, however, that offspring from a mating whose production was spread over several years would show a relatively
constant proportion of successes. We searched, therefore, for
dams and sires who had progeny in successive years between 1958
and 1962 and compared the changes in success of their offspring
with the trend in the much larger total population. The results
were incontrovertible. In eight separate comparisons the direction of change among the offspring of these parents was the
same as that in the total population, made up largely of non-
repeated matings. The fluctuations were so great when the
stock was kept constant that it seems unnecessary to invoke a
genetic explanation for them.

Unfortunately, our analysis cannot define or even clearly
suggest the nongenetic factors which must have operated over
the years 1958-1962. Possibly a relatively smaller supply of
dogs of the 1962 whelp in relation to the need led to greater
effort by the trainers to develop marginal subjects. The implication of nongenetic factors in major fluctuations of percentage of success in training does not mean that heredity plays
little part in the success of a guide dog. The present analysis does demonstrate that large changes can occur even when
heredity is held constant and suggests conservatism in accepting genetic explanations.

Production and Age of Breeding Stock

It is well known that reproductive vigor declines with
age. Hence, animal breeders generally retire their breeding
stock on a schedule to optimize production. To determine the
effect of age of breeding stock upon the production of guide
dogs, all records were classified according to the age of sire
at time of birth. Separate analyses were made for each of the

Table 9.5

AGE OF BITCH AND PRODUCTIVITY

Age of Bitch at Mating Months	Number Matings	Number Litters Born	Percent Fertile	Mean Litter Size Birth	8 wk.	Percent Survival	Prod. Index[*]
7-18	51	33	65	7.5	5.4	72	3.5
19-30	77	58	75	7.6	5.9	78	4.4
31-42	69	50	72	8.4	6.5	77	4.7
43-54	60	45	75	8.1	5.7	70	4.3
55-66	47	42	89	7.9	5.7	72	5.1
67-78	23	21	91	8.6	5.3	62	4.9
79-90	23	17	74	6.8	4.0	59	3.0
91-102	6	5	83	5.8	4.2	72	3.5
103-114	4	2	50	5.5	4.5	82	2.2

[*]The Production Index is the average number of puppies per mating reaching the age of eight weeks.

major breeds. No consistent effects of the age of sire were detected. However, a similar analysis for effects of age in bitches showed a definite reduction in productivity in females whelping before 18 months or over 78 months of age. Since the phenomenon appeared to be similar in all breeds, the data from the three breeds have been summarized together in Table 9.5.

This table was based upon observed matings of 223 German shepherds, 67 golden retrievers and 56 Labrador retrievers in the period January 1, 1957, to June 30, 1965. From these 360 matings were born 273 litters, yielding a fertility rate of 76%. Fertility held up well to 102 months, but only two litters resulted from four matings in bitches over this age. The number was too small to be meaningful. Mean litter size fell in litters whelped by bitches over 78 months (6½ years) of age. The survival rate of puppies born to older mothers was little, if any, lower than that of puppies from young mothers. Thus the reduced productivity of the older bitches shown in the right-hand column of Table 9.5 is ascribable primarily to lower litter size; fertility and maternal care seem to be relatively unimpaired. Of course these bitches may have been retained as breeders beyond the normal age of retirement because they were exceptionally productive.

On the basis of these data it would be recommended that bitches of these stocks be retired from breeding at the age of six years. Other stocks of the same breeds and other breeds may vary somewhat, but in general, fertility in bitches begins to decline at 5-5½ years. Exceptions should be made only to insure perpetuation of a particularly desired line. Sires can be used as long as they are sexually competent, and particularly good sires should be retained as long as possible.

A study was also made of the later history of the offspring of 20 German shepherd bitches who produced a series of litters, some before and some after five years of age. The data are shown in Table 9.6). Offspring of the youngest mothers were most likely to succeed, as 34% became guide dogs. When only dogs entering training were considered (2 lower rows in Table 9.6) the differences in success among the groups reached significance (Chi-square = 10.00; d.f. = 3; p = .02). Bitches whelping at 3-4 years produced pups 6% poorer than the younger group, and a further decline of 6% took place in the next oldest group. The upturn in the offspring of the oldest bitches runs against the conclusion that older mothers produced poorer pups, but the numbers involved were quite small, and their success may have been the result of retaining only unusually good bitches to this age. Furthermore, the previously demonstrated annual fluctuations in training success, which appear to reflect variations in supply and demand (and possibly in kennel management), should induce caution in interpreting the observed variations as an age-of-dam effect. At any rate, it would be economically undesirable to retire bitches after only one or two litters, especially since the decline becomes important only at 5-6 years. It would be of great theoretical interest to continue observations on the training success of successive litters from the same dam to see whether any systematic effect can be detected

Table 9.6

AGE OF DAM AND SUCCESS OF OFFSPRING IN TRAINING

		Dam's Age in Years at Whelping			
		1-2	3-4	5-6	7-8
Pups Born	Number	176	225	217	38
Died Before 8 Weeks	Number	46	47	80	14
	Percent	26	21	37	37
Other Loss Prior to Training	Number	31	39	33	4
	Percent	18	22	15	10
Saved for Breeding	Number	18	13	13	3
	Percent	10	6	6	8
Rejects - Training	Number	21	·54	43	6
	Percent	12	24	20	16
Became Guides	Number	60	62	48	11
	Percent	34	28	22	29

with a larger sample, especially since achievement in human
families declines from first borns to children born later in
the same family (Belmont & Marolla, 1973).

Use of Donated Dogs

Guide Dogs for the Blind has trained and placed many dogs
not of its own breeding. In the early days of the institution
donations were a major source of supply. One must be careful
in comparing the performance of such animals with those raised
in the standard guide dog system. Perhaps the most meaningful
comparison is restricted to the proportions of dogs entering
training who are rejected for behavioral reasons and who qualify as guides. In the decade 1941-1950 the records show that
374 donated dogs provided 118 guides (30.7%). During the same
period 271 dogs from Guide Dogs for the Blind breeding entered
training and provided 76 guides (28.0). The proportion of success is similar in the two groups within the limits of sampling
errors.

In the following decade, 1951-1960, the proportion of donated dogs fell although the total number, 363, was nearly as
high as in the previous ten years. From these donations, 200
guide dogs (55.0%) were obtained. During the same period 797
Guide Dogs for the Blind dogs who entered training yielded 485
guides (62.1%). On the face of the evidence, improvements in
training procedure must be given credit for the advance, since
both donated and Guide Dogs for the Blind bred dogs shared in
the increased success (Figure 3.1). However, the matter is not
that simple. Because of bad experience with donated animals,
all offered dogs were observed and given preliminary training
before being accepted. Hence, the recorded donations are an
unknown fraction of the offered animals. The data do demonstrate that donated dogs can be selected so that over half of
the selectees can become guides. This is not surprising, since
all of the procedures used in the School's rearing and pretrain-
ing programs can be employed by private breeders. Furthermore,
the Guide Dogs for the Blind stock has no monopoly on superior
genotypes. Nevertheless, the institutional policy of depending
primarily upon its own animals is commendable, since control of
the entire procedure is essential to assure a supply of suitable
dogs for training when they are needed.

In the final section of this chapter we present a breeding
program for the continuous replacement of the stock. Here we
shall be concerned only with the quantitative aspects of the
breeding plan. The choice of selection indices is considered
in other chapters.

Planning for Replacement

The data presented in this chapter form the basis for a
recommendended program of setting aside breeding stock to maximize production of guide dogs. The assumption is made that the
results of the better years will continue to be achieved in the
future. Should major improvements be made in survival of infant pups or in the percentage of dogs qualifying during training, adjustments could be made. These recommendations are
based on experience with Guide Dogs for the Blind as conditions
existed at the time this study was made, but similar considera-

tions should apply to any similar institution.

We start with a requirement of 8 guide dogs per month for assignment to students.* If we assume that one-half the animals brought into training will qualify, 16 dogs must start training each month. On the average 20 pups must be placed in 4-H homes to provide 16 year-old dogs. To produce these 20 pups, approximately 27 pups must be born, based on an average survival of about 75%. For protection against heavier loss at certain times, a slightly larger goal is desirable. One expects somewhat over 7 pups per litter; hence 4 litters per month should be adequate. However, only four-fifths of matings result in litters, thus 5 to 6 matings must be made monthly to insure 4 litters. Some leeway in the requirement for matings is provided by dogs that are returned after a short period of service and are available for reissue. Our estimate does not allow for these animals, which may be regarded as insurance against losses greater than the average.

If each breeding bitch is mated once annually, it will require 60 to 72 of them to meet the requirements for guide dog production. The numerical requirement for sires is less critical; 12 to 15 should be adequate. We have seen that the optimum breeding period of a bitch spans five years, ages 2 to 7. Hence, one-fifth of the breeding bitches should be replaced each year. Although the useful life of a sire is somewhat longer, we shall estimate that one-fifth of the sires should be replaced annually. Thus, the annual requirement for breeding stock replacement is 12 to 15 bitches and 2 to 4 sires, a little better than one dog per month. If the number of matings is somewhat on the generous side (6 per month) and losses are held within average limits, this recommended program will supply breeding stock requirements adequately.

For the long-range welfare of an institution and of its

---

*In 1976, classes of 16 students were being taught at Guide Dogs for the Blind, double the numbers that could be handled in the early days of the institution, and requiring double the numbers used in these production figures. Possibly for this reason, donated dogs (mostly puppies) were being used in large numbers, although they have the disadvantage of not forming a regular supply.

blind students, breeding stock replacement should have priority
in times of shortage of dogs. Failure to replace breeding stock
on schedule can lead to chronic rather than temporary shortages
of dogs. If an institution grows, it must plan for enlargement
of the breeding stock in proportion to the anticipated increase
in demand. If data such as have been presented here are available, planning can be as precise as is ever possible when dealing with biological systems.

References

Belmont, L. & Marolla, F. A. Birth order, family size, and
    intelligence. Science, 1973, 182, 1096-1101.
Corbin, J. E., Mohrman, R. K. & Wilke, H. L. Purebred dogs in
    nutrition research. Proc. Animal Care Panel, 1962, 12,
    163-168.
Scott, J. P. & Fuller, J. L. Genetics and the Social Behavior
    of the Dog. Chicago: University of Chicago Press, 1965.

LOOKING TO THE FUTURE

J. P. Scott, J. L. Fuller and S. W. Bielfelt

The studies described in this book were undertaken for two general purposes. One was to analyze the program at Guide Dogs for the Blind and to try to discover ways in which the production of desirable guide dogs could be increased. The second purpose, and one which is perhaps even more important, was to provide a model for other similar institutions, especially those that may be set up in the future for rearing and training guide dogs.

In the course of this research four general problems have developed, relating respectively to early experience, the prediction of future success, the improvement of behavior and physique through selective breeding, and the economics of guide dog production.

What is the Most Desirable Sort of
Early Experience for a Guide Dog?

From the questionnaire research analyzed in Chapter 5, we concluded that there are certain general principles that should be followed in programming the care and preliminary training that puppies receive in foster homes prior to being trained as guide dogs. A puppy should be given as wide experiences as possible, and always under favorable circumstances, i.e., in which the puppy is not frightened or hurt. Among these experiences, it is essential that he be exposed to the general kind of environment in which he will later live, which is usually that of a home and streets of an urban community. However, dogs reared in a rural environment and allowed to roam freely, and country dogs that were regularly taken into towns or cities on leash, performed better than dogs reared in towns and cities or kept at home. We therefore recommend that the 4-H trainers of puppies be encouraged to provide free running experience and expeditions to towns on leash for their dogs whenever possible, and that rural homes be given preference in the placement of puppies. Some other minor considerations in placement are to avoid homes in which the family is habitually away all day or places the puppy in boarding kennels for long periods.

Other than these minor modifications, the most important problem, and one for which this research gives no precise solution, is whether the general system of rearing should or should not be modified. As it was practiced during the years when this research was conducted, the dogs were kept in kennels from birth until 12 weeks, when they were put into foster homes. If they were retained in the kennels longer than 12 weeks, as frequently happened in the very early stages of the guide dog program, their performance as guides suffered. Could the percentage of successful animals be increased even further by placing puppies in foster homes earlier than 12 weeks? Recent experience with shifting the entire puppy testing and training program to 6-10 weeks has been favorable, although no precise statistics are available.

We also have theoretical reasons for believing that further modifications might be useful. Research done at the Jackson Laboratory and later at Bowling Green University leads to the following conclusions concerning behavioral development in the dog:

The period between 3 and 12 weeks of age is critical for the establishment of normal social relationships with human beings, and also for attachment to a particular physical locality. The optimum time for removing a puppy from the kennel, switching it to a different environment and allowing it to form an attachment to a human family is between 6 and 8 weeks of age. Twelve weeks (the time when puppies were formerly placed in 4-H homes in the guide dog program) is therefore close to the upper limit of the critical period and well above the optimal time. If these research findings can be transferred into practice, they indicate that guide dog puppies should be placed in the foster homes at approximately 8 weeks of age rather than at 12.

Such a procedural change would, however, interfere with

the testing program. Under the system described in this book,
the 8 to 12 week period is used to test the aptitudes of puppies.
As indicated in the analysis of these tests (See Chapter 3),
little is gained by repeating these tests over a period of
several weeks, as the best predictability of future success in
most cases is obtained early in the testing program. We estimate that the loss in information brought about by such a change
would be unimportant.

The testing program, however, has another aspect. Once a
week each puppy is taken out of the kennel individually and exposed to a variety of human handlers. It is possible that this
provides a kind of experience essential for good adjustment as
a guide dog. We would predict that under these circumstances
a puppy would become attached to no one particular person, but
rather to human beings in general. This should have useful
results, as the future guide dog must later be able to switch
this attachment from the 4-H trainer and caretakers to the
guide dog trainer and then again to his blind master without
becoming seriously upset emotionally. The testing experience
also gives, in a very slight degree, some experience with the
outside world that the puppy will eventually meet. Could the
4-H program provide the same sort of experience?

There is always risk in changing a system which is func-
tioning reasonably well. Such changes may have effects which
are totally unforeseen at the outset. Because of this risk,
we would propose an experimental approach to the problem, using
a relatively small sample of puppies and not disclosing to the
trainers what their experience had been. The plan would be to
take several litters and divide each into three groups. The
first, or control group, would be tested from 6 to 10 weeks in
the now current system and put out immediately thereafter. The
second group would be given the puppy testing program from 6 to
9 weeks only, and be assigned to 4-H homes at 9 weeks. The
third group would be given the puppy testing from 6 to 8 weeks
and then be placed in homes immediately thereafter. Allowing
for the usual attrition for other than behavioral reasons, a
final total of 25 puppies in each group would be satisfactory.

Our prediction would be that if it is beneficial to take
the puppies out of the kennels sooner, the 8-week old group

would be best, the 9-week old group second best, and the 10-week old poorest when they came to final training. If there are conflicting beneficial effects in that early removal from the kennel is good but also that the testing experience is helpful, we would predict that the best combination of the two would be produced by removal at 10 weeks. Aside from the benefits to the puppies, any shortening of the period in the kennel should result in the saving of money to a guide dog organization, since the cost of rearing in the foster homes is not borne by the institution but by private individuals.

A final recommendation concerns the age at which the prospective guide dogs are brought in for training. According to the standard system, dogs were supposed to be returned to the kennel by their 4-H raisers by the age of 12 months. Owing to fluctuations in the supply and demand for dogs, there was actually considerable variation in age, as much as two months ahead of the standard time, or three months later. Examination of the records of these dogs showed that there was no difference in performance that was related to age.

While trainers and dog owners generally have the impression that dogs settle down and become easier to work with after sexual maturity, there is no evidence that age differences in beginning training affected the outcome of training in these particular dogs. Records were not available that would show which dogs were trained before and which dogs after sexual maturity, and we can only conclude that the present system of initiating final training at anywhere from 10 to 15 months is satisfactory.

Attempting to train all puppies as early as 10 months would result in some saving of time and expense to the persons who rear the dogs in the foster homes but would not directly benefit the guide dog organization itself. The only real saving would be in those cases where a 4-H member took on another puppy immediately after turning over the old one to Guide Dogs for the Blind. However, this happens relatively infrequently, as such a project is usually a one-time affair for most children. Furthermore, there is some evidence that repeat puppies do not do as well as the first one that a child trains.

<u>Improvement by Selection</u>

<u>Physical characteristics</u>. Selection for size and conforma-
tion is a relatively easy task, because such measurements as
weight and height can be done with great accuracy, and are relatively little affected by environment provided all animals are
receiving adequate nutrition. As Chapters 7 and 8 show, the
selection program did affect the guide dogs, resulting in the
development of relatively compact animals with straight legs and
normally standing fully upright. The effects were greatest in
the German shepherd breed because many shepherds in the original
stock were much larger than is desirable for a guide dog, and
the selection program reduced them to a more useful size. The
retrievers, which were of a desirable height to begin with, were
chiefly affected in the reduction of body length, so that they
consequently became more compact and blocky in appearance than
the original stock. Fuller (Chapter 7) also showed that the
measurements could be reduced to a simplified set of 5--weight,
muzzle length, standing height, tail length, and body length.

Other than this, the principal problem of physique was the
occurrence of hip dysplasia. Lameness was an important defect,
and resulted in considerable losses prior to the time of training. However, many animals that appeared to have defective hips,
as shown by X-rays, did not develop lameness, and performed adequately as guide dogs. Ginsburg's study indicates that this
defect could be eliminated by selective breeding, provided a detailed X-ray analysis is used to detect all possible defects,
including minor ones.

<u>Selection for improved behavior</u>. This is a far more diffi-
cult task to accomplish than selection for physique, partly
because environmental factors as well as genetic ones can be
very important, and partly because of the complex nature of behavior, which involves the animal's organizing a large number
of capacities to produce an integrated performance. As a dog
does this, it may well compensate for a weakness in one trait
by employing a strength in another, with the result that two
dogs that appear to give equally good performance in training
may actually be quite different in their basic behavioral capacities. It would be ideal if we could develop a stock of animals that were pure breeding for a group of capacities that

would be desirable under all conditions, but without knowing what these capacities are and how they are inherited we can only select for the final result.

As the statistics show, selection was accompanied by a great improvement in performance over the first few years of the program. Unfortunately for the purposes of pure science, the same period was accompanied by a strong improvement in the whole program of care and training, so that it is difficult to assess how much each contributed to the final result. Presumably both selection and improved training methods did have an effect, but one of the disappointing things was that after the initial improvement the average success ratio of the dogs that were trained remained stable at about 60-66%.

Selection was done in two ways. One used the puppy tests as a criterion for selecting breeding stock by choosing those puppies which performed most adequately on the tests. Following this and accompanying it, there was a marked improvement in the puppy testing scores, giving definite evidence that the selection program was effective. There were some objections to this interpretation on the grounds that the puppy testers might have relaxed their standards as the years went on. This explanation was rejected on the ground that not all tests showed such changes, and that the biggest changes occurred in those tests that were given most weight in the selection process. We concluded that the puppies in the later years were indeed genetically better than those in the earlier years.

It would have been better to select animals for breeding on the basis of actual guide dog performance, but since animals were normally castrated before training, this method was obviously impractical. Another method that could be used, and was actually used, in addition to the puppy testing program, was that of progeny testing. One animal in particular, the German shepherd Frank of Ledge Acres, was repeatedly used as a sire because of the excellence of his offspring.

If we were to do a similar program again, progeny testing would obviously be a superior method. It is costly, since it requires the progeny to be raised to maturity and trained, irrespective of their quality. Only experience would show whether the results would compensate for the added expense.

Puppy testing could be used in combination with this, as indeed it was, to weed out defective and obviously incompetent puppies.

The result of an effective selection program should be to produce animals that have a combination of physical and behavioral traits that facilitate guide dog training. As we stated above, there may be many equally good combinations, and there may be diverse ways by which such a combination can be attained, specific deficiencies being compensated for by other strengths. The offspring of parents with different basic characteristics may not inherit the proper match and thus fail to meet requirements. Thus we would predict the kind of result that was actually achieved, namely, that a perfect group of guide dogs was never produced.

Further progress through selection could only be achieved by the identification of the special abilities and capacities that make up one very superior combination. With this information it might be possible to develop a relatively pure breeding stock which produced only high quality offspring. As things stand, continual selection must be practiced, not merely to achieve improvement, but to maintain the quality of the stock.

Early selection on the basis of puppy tests. The puppy tests were not perfect predictors of adult performance as guide dogs, although they give as good or better results than corresponding tests that attempt to predict human performance. However, our analysis showed that their predictive value could be improved in two ways: by changing the basis of scoring and giving certain sub-tests more weight than others; and by introducing new tests that would specifically deal with the traits for which trainers most frequently discard guide dogs, namely shyness and distractibility.

Our results showed that the tests that gave the best predictive results were those involved in elementary obedience training: Sit, Come, Fetch, and Heel, with special emphasis on Fetch and Heel. Also, the test scores that gave the best predictability were those obtained from the first or second trials. Another group that gave important results included tests of emotional arousal to various stimuli. These are closely related to the shyness and timidity that are major reasons for discarding adult dogs in training. An unexpected result was that there appear to be important maternal effects on the expression of these tests of emotional arousal. Such effects should be reflected in the progeny tests, along with genetic effects, and thus be useful in any selection program. A field for future research will be to try to discover how the mothers affect their offspring. In the 4-H program it appeared, contrary to what one might expect, that a shy family dog resulted in a more confident guide dog.

Using the puppy test to discard potentially poor performers should be continued. Our results showed that a poor performing puppy had only an even chance of success, while a failed puppy had only 1 chance in 4. Discarding these animals early has undoubtedly saved a great deal of disappointment on the part of the 4-H puppy raisers, and considerable time and expense for the trainers.

Possible use of F_1 hybrids. Unlike agriculturists, dog breeders and managers have never taken advantage of the obvious benefits of crossing two pure strains and using only the first generation hybrids. This technique has revolutionized the production of maize and is now being extensively used in the poultry industry.

As practiced commercially, the first step was to develop a variety of inbred strains of corn, and then by experimental crossing between them discover which crosses gave the best results. The advantages rest on the fact that F_1 hybrids are genetically as uniform as their inbred parents and thus, with respect to appearance, or phenotype, the hybrids are as uniform or even more uniform than the parent strains, facilitating their harvest by machinery. More importantly, the hybrids show heterosis, or hybrid vigor, and are immensely more productive than any random bred strain or even the best selected strains.

As applied to dogs, it would be at present impractical to try to develop inbred strains, because of the large scale breeding project that would have to be undertaken without any hope of commercial repayment. Without inbred strains, one can not hope to get the degree of uniformity that is present in hybrid corn, but one can still reap the benefits of hybrid vigor by

breed crossing. As they now exist, the various pure breeds are
riddled with injurious recessive genes that reduce the fertility and health of the animals. We have found that crosses between breeds, particularly if they are between widely unrelated
breeds, cancel out most of the recessives with the result that
the hybrids are remarkably healthy and vigorous animals. For
example, in our studies of crosses between cocker spaniels and
basenjis, the neonatal mortality was reduced from approximately
13% (the average of the two pure breeds) to approximately 3%,
a reduction of about 75% (Scott & Fuller, 1965). Furthermore,
the hybrids were tough, vigorous animals that would survive
under almost any conditions, even when the purebred mother took
poor and ineffective care of them. As adults they were beautifully healthy and vigorous animals. Some of them were so gifted
physically that they could even scale the 7-foot fences that we
had erected around their runs.

Since then we have made some small scale studies of hybrid-
ization in other breeds. F_1 hybrids between Telomians and Shetland sheep dogs turned out to be exceptionally healthy, as might
be expected, and almost unusually gifted with respect to training (Scott, et al., 1973). They performed better than either
pure bred parent strain on three out of four training tasks, and
on one of them, a complex discrimination test in the Wisconsin
General Testing apparatus, they performed like veritable geni-
uses, outdoing even the rhesus monkeys for whom the test was
originally devised.

As applied to guide dog production, we would recommend
experimental crosses between the three breeds that have been
found successful: German shepherds, Labradors, and golden
retrievers. None of these breeds are closely related, and
there should be a marked reduction in mortality and a great
improvement in physical health as a minimum result.

Since the largest single cause of loss is puppy death,
42% of all losses during one previous period (See Table 9.2)
the saving would be considerable. Which crosses would turn out
best from the viewpoint of training would have to be determined
by experience, but since all three breeds have been shown to be
equally successful in guide dog training, we would predict that
the crosses would at least show less variability than the pure

strains and therefore achieve higher average success, and also
that there would be a good probability that the ceiling of performance would be raised with an even greater reduction of
trainer time and effort.

From the viewpoint of practical logistics, after experiments had shown which is the most desirable cross, only two
breeds would need to be maintained. Enough purebred matings
would have to be made to maintain the necessary number of brood
bitches at the optimum number of 100-120, based on previous
operations. Since most females must be retired after 5 years,
this means producing 20-25 of them each year for brood bitches
alone. A similar number of males would necessarily be produced,
and most of these could be used as guides, since only 10-12
sires would be needed for the whole colony, requiring replacements of perhaps 2 per year.

The purebred stock could thus be maintained by breeding
approximately 10 litters per year, leaving the rest of the females available for hybrid production. Experience might well
show that the total number of bitches could be reduced. If
such a program is undertaken, it should be monitored by a professional geneticist, preferably one sophisticated in behavioral
genetics, in order to avoid pitfalls of excessive inbreeding in
the pure stocks and to maintain effective selection programs.

There might be some problems connected with size, as the
hybrids would tend to be somewhat larger, but this could be
compensated for by selecting moderate-sized parents. The other
disadvantage that might be anticipated arises from the fact that
good-looking dogs are necessary for developing confidence in
blind people, who are often very sensitive to criticism with
respect to their own personal appearance and also those of their
dogs. Such criticisms as the question, "What kind of dog is
that?" could be countered by giving the hybrids a unique name
and also by pointing out their special uses and reputation.
For example, a hybrid might be called a "Hyguide", or perhaps
"Superguide". As to beauty, the three breeds chosen are not
dissimilar in appearance, and would be unlikely to produce
freakish-looking offspring. In a Labrador-German shepherd
cross, the Labrador characteristics would be dominant in color,
hair length and ear carriage, and the hybrids might well resem-

ble unusually handsome and vigorous Labradors. Since short hair
is dominant, this would be an advantage for ease of care. A
Labrador-golden retriever cross involves more similar characteristics, and the F_1 hybrid might well be almost indistinguishable
from a Labrador.

The Monetary Aspects of Guide Dog Production

Raising and training guide dogs is necessarily an expensive process, but one which is eminently rewarding both to the
blind persons who benefit and to those individuals who contribute time and money to the process. As alternatives, there have
been attempts to develop sensing machines that would replace
the guide dog, and many blind persons still depend on canes
for getting around. For others, however, the guide dog has an
immense advantage over machines or mechanical devices in that
the dog provides constant companionship, a greater sense of
independence, and the confidence that comes from company without
the dependence that results from being led by a human companion.

Nevertheless, any economies that can be made in either
money or effort will at the very least make it possible to ex-
tend the benefits of guide dog training to more individuals.
We have already indicated above two points where savings might
be made following suitable experimentation. That of reducing
the length of stay of the puppies in the kennels below 12 weeks
is somewhat doubtful, since it may turn out that the experience
of contact with a number of strange people outside the kennel
during the testing program is more desirable than shifting
immediately to a family. Also, the time and money saved would
be relatively small. On the other hand, the F_1 hybrid program
could be predicted to have a high probability of success in
reducing both neonatal mortality and training failures, which
are the biggest causes of losses.

As Fuller shows in his chapter on logistics, the German
shepherds and Labrador retrievers used at the time this study
was made were regularly losing one third of their puppies, which
is a rate at least twice as high as the average of 15% which one
expects in pure bred dogs. Using F_1 hybrids might well reduce
this rate from 33 percent to 4 or 5%. As Fuller points out,

reducing the infantile death rate by even half would enable the breeding stock to be reduced by 13%, which would be no small saving in these days when feeding and basic care of an adult dog of this size is likely to cost at least $1.00 a day, even in a favorable climate like that of California.

Another route is to improve the quality and availability of veterinary care. We have found that the most dangerous period for survival of young puppies is within the first 3 days after birth, and that corrective measures are most effective if applied during the first few hours. Guide Dogs for the Blind now has a resident veterinarian and can provide such care. Survival statistics are undoubtedly much better today than when this study was made. However, such care can only go so far in helping weak and defective puppies, and may even do harm in the long run if such puppies are genetically defective and used as breeding stock. Selection for the capacity to produce healthy puppies is an essential element in any breeding program.

Analyzing costs under the system used at Guide Dogs for the Blind, the principal expenses are for the maintenance of brood bitches and stud dogs, the rearing of pups, the supervision of pups in the 4-H program, and in the final testing and training program. Of these the 4-H program is the least expensive in terms of cash outlay, because services and care of the dogs are almost entirely contributed by volunteers. The final training of the guide dogs and their future masters is of course the most expensive part of the whole program. Therefore most money can be saved by increasing the efficiency of the training program.

There are several ways in which this ideal can be approached, but we should remember that no human system and no canine system will ever give perfect results, and that this is a goal toward which work can be directed rather than one which could ever be achieved completely.

In the first place, the available animals can be improved by a selection program. Any selection program is likely to achieve maximum results in 4 or 5 generations, and the evidence from the San Rafael experience was that this result was achieved rather early in the program, and that relatively little if any improvement occurred in later years. Further improvement can be expected only by adding other selection criteria, particularly against those traits which cause the biggest losses in training, such as nervousness and distractibility (See Chapter 3). In any case, constant selection must be kept up in order to maintain the stocks.

As we have suggested, very considerable improvement might be achieved by using these selected strains to produce F_1 hybrids. This is almost the only way in which animals could be boosted above the selected level, and has the advantage of achieving very quick results.

Second, the analysis of the results of the 4-H program indicate that certain changes and improvements in the way in which this program is administered might result in savings of 5 or 10% of the number of dogs that become successful. This would mean moving from the current optimum figures of around 66% to perhaps 75% of success. One of the obvious factors is the skill of the children as dog trainers, and this skill can be improved by training the children and selecting those who do the best.

Finally, as Fuller concludes in Chapter 9, there was considerable fluctuation of results from year to year during a period when the dog strains should have been made relatively uniform by selection. This suggests that environmental factors were contributing to the success or failure of the dogs. There are two obvious courses for improving the environment. One is that of experimenting with improved methods of training. The study made in this book was primarily one of investigating the effects of genetics, and we assumed that the trainers were using the best possible methods, and that every effort was made to secure and train high quality human personnel. Certainly this was being done at the time we studied the program. Nevertheless, it would probably pay to do some research on the nature of training methods used, with a view to possible modification. Operant conditioning procedures have found important application in educating children and eliminating undesirable behavior patterns at any age. The procedures have also been applied to animal training for circuses, movies and TV shows. It is likely that they would find an application in the training of guide dogs, especially if the trainers were instructed in the princi-

ples involved. Present methods based on years of practical experience produce many excellent guides, but it seems likely to
us that improvement is still possible. Research in this area
would be relatively inexpensive to do, and there are many animal
psychologists who would be capable of directing it. Finally,
and this almost goes without saying, every effort should be made
to maintain the high morale and level of competence among the
trainers themselves.

Conclusion

We cannot write the final part of this book without saying
something about the personal side of our experience. For most
of us, this was a first venture into applied research. Although
much of our other scientific work was basic to various medical
problems, we had never before made a direct effort to analyze
and solve a purely practical problem. In attempting to do this
we have developed a new appreciation of the difficulties and
problems of applied research, especially if that research deals
with people.

Like any problem of human affairs, this was an interdisci-
plinary one. Our own basic training had been primarily in
biology and genetics, and here we were confronted with the
solution of a problem that obviously involved applied human
sociology and social psychology. If enough time and money had
been available, we could very profitably have used an even
larger team of researchers. As it was, we had to develop our
own knowledge and resources in the social sciences, and one of
our realizations was that in any scientific work dealing with
human behavior someone has to do a tremendous job in human relations.

In our case we were extremely lucky to find ourselves
dealing with a staff and volunteers who understood and apprec-
iated what we were trying to do, and were helpful and friendly
at all times. The day-to-day difficulties that were inevitable
in trying to fit a scientific investigation into a busy and
intensely important practical operation were immensely aided
by our having the late C. J. Pfaffenberger on our team. His
constant effort, and his immense gift for creating an atmosphere

of friendly good-will around our enterprise, smoothed our way
immeasurably. He was ably assisted by Sherman Bielfelt, who
was the one of us who was constantly at hand to represent the
guide dog research project, and who was able to operate extra-
ordinarily efficiently without giving offense.

Besides the possibility of interfering with on-going work,
there is another difficulty, in that the essence of the scientific method is reducing observable facts into impersonal figures,
and people do not like to have their behavior looked at coldly
and impersonally. They feel, and correctly so, that something
has been left out--namely the warm interpersonal contact that
makes life rewarding. With some success we applied the team
approach to this problem. While some of us were being objective
and impersonal, others were supplying the personal interaction.

In this particular venture we were primarily concerned with
the human+dog relationship and devoted most of our attention to
the canine half of the relationship. If more research were to
be done in the future, equal attention ought to be placed on
the human side of the relationship, for our experience has
shown that while the human+dog relationship is an excellent
model for the human parent+child relationship, the effects go
in both directions. Although the human master controls his dog,
his dog also controls him in ways that are not yet completely
understood. It is this fact that lies at the heart of the
problem of whether guide dogs could or should be replaced by
mechanical sensing devices.

For all of us, this research was outside and in addition
to our personal career-based efforts, and it is for this reason
that until now none of it has been presented to an audience
of scientists. In addition, the problem eventually turned out
to be far more complex and difficult than anyone realized at
the beginning. Although we have all contributed a great deal
of time other than that for which we were regularly employed,
we were able to do our extra work on it only when there was
time to spare from our own pressing concerns. Finally, Pfaffenberger's death on September 9, 1967, slowed our progress, not
so much because he had left anything undone, but because his encouragement and enthusiasm provided a driving force for the
whole enterprise. In recognition and gratitude for his efforts

and insight in getting an important scientific enterprise off
the ground, we hope this book will be a lasting monument to his
memory.

References

Scott, J. P. and Fuller, J. L. Genetics and the Social Behavior
    of the Dog. Chicago: University of Chicago Press, 1965.
Scott, J. P., Stewart, J. M. and DeGhett, V. J. Separation in
    infant dogs. In: J. P. Scott and E. C. Senay (Eds.),
    Separation and Depression. Washington, D.C., American
    Association for the Advancement of Science, 1973.

INDEX